CAPs 101:

Basic
Competencies,
Attributes and
Practices of
Leaders and Managers

Copyright 2023 KH Meyers
Printed in the United States
All Rights reserved

Reproduction of any portion of this book in any form is prohibited without authorization. The author appreciates the reader's respect for the copyright laws. Requests for permission to reproduce any of the material contained in this book can be directed to: khmeyers2021@gmail.com.

Printed using Kindle Direct Publishing
USA

Copies can be ordered directly from Amazon by searching the title or the author: KH Meyers

ISBN   979-8-9865026-4-9

CAPs 101:

Basic
Competencies,
Attributes, and
Practices
of Leaders or Managers

KH Meyers

Introduction

Background

Welcome to CAPs 101: The Basic **C**ompetencies, **A**ttributes and **P**ractices of Leaders and Managers. It is my sincere hope that the information in this book provides you with a functioning knowledge of skills inherent in good leadership or management. (I will use the terms leadership and management interchangeably throughout, though there are some very clear, meaningful distinctions between the two in practice.)

It doesn't matter if you are on the first or top rung of the corporate ladder, or striving to succeed as a budding entrepreneur, leadership in any capacity is leadership and there are some identifiable skills that, if studied and practiced, will serve you well. It is my belief that if you learn them thoroughly, look for them in leaders within your circles of influence, and then put them into practice yourself, these CAPs will form a solid backdrop from which to succeed.

So, who am I to tell you about leadership or management? Good question. For 25 years I was the manager/leader of a building with over 100 employees and thousands of clients. It was a middle level leadership position within a system of several such buildings, thousands of employees and an enormous number of clients. I answered to a supervisor who monitored my performance and the production at my building.

I was, in fact, a school principal. That's right, a school principal. But before you dismiss my qualifications to write about leadership, I think you would have to agree that as a principal I needed to delegate with the same effectiveness as the CEO of a Fortune 500 company. I was expected to manage interaction among staff just as efficiently as any state governor. And I had to monitor my building's reputation with the same voracity as the owner of a local bakery.

Running a school was a big part of my professional career. Because of my interest in leadership, I obtained a doctorate in Educational Leadership with a focus on teacher evaluation. I was awarded by the

Commissioner of Education a medal for being the most effective Elementary Principal in Central Florida. And as a consultant, I was paid to rate leadership skill levels of prospective candidates applying for school administrative positions in various school districts around the state.

Serving as a consultant and interviewing hundreds of candidates hoping to become administrators throughout the state was rewarding and interesting. I was introduced to a set of leadership competencies back in the 1980's at a Management Training Institute for school principals. It was there I was introduced to the 19 principal competencies by Snyder and Drummond. I was later certified as one of just a limited number of evaluators in the state to identify and rate the attainment level of the competencies in applicants for school or district leadership positions. I have probably logged thousands of hours evaluating the skill levels of aspiring candidates for school administrator positions, even after retirement.

Your next question is probably, "Why this set of skills?" Another good question. As I said earlier, to me leadership is leadership and the skills needed to lead effectively don't change. The more knowledgeable you are regarding these foundational, proven skills, the more likely you set yourself up for success. Just as there are basic skills that need to be learned in any endeavor, there are basic skills that need to be mastered if you are going to be in charge. The research is abundant regarding the existence and worth of these basic skills.

Too, as I continued my own interest in leadership by attending seminars and conferences, I could always find a link from the "newest" leadership theories right back to one or more of these 19 CAPs. I am sure there are new models of leadership that will be identified as it is further studied, but these 19 serve as a very strong and long-lasting foundation. Any new discoveries on leadership qualities or behaviors, based on my experience, will fit comfortably within or alongside one or more of these. I am not suggesting there is nothing more to learn in this area. You might consider this list a primer. Yet it will provide you with reliable, operative, and effective tools if leadership or management is your career goal.

If you picked up this book because you aspire to higher position, or are already there and want to become more effective, I think you will find it worth the minimal cost, at least. But even more, I hope you find these 19 CAPs applicable. Though basic, they offer a solid foundation on which to build a career in leadership.

Disclaimer

This book is not written to be a textbook, though I am sure a very effective course on basic leadership skills could be designed around its content in any college field from education to engineering—I would more characterize it as self-help. This is as much checking off an item on my bucket list as it is anything else. This information has been sitting on my computer and in notebooks for years. I have long thought they were important enough to reorganize and put them out there for others to consider and learn. Having acknowledged that, after reading and editing the content several times, there may still be some imperfect use of words, or an extra or missing comma. Just take that into consideration. (If you find needed changes—like those missing commas—feel to let me know so I can correct the content. I would appreciate an email at khmeyers2021@gmail.com. It is my desire to not only present the information, but to do so to the best of my ability.) This is a personal as opposed to an academic contribution to the field of leadership and hope you will appreciate it as such.

Finally, you will find there is overlap between CAPs in some areas. The CAP, "Take-Charge" Mentality will have some overlap with "Making Decisions", for example. While they are all fairly individualistic, parts of one may sound or look like parts of another. It is natural in that they are all behavioristic. Don't let that take you off course or dismiss the opportunity to learn each one.

Thank you for taking a chance on this book. I would love to hear back from you regarding any part of it.

KH Meyers

Preface

Before I jump right into the 19 CAPs, I want to share briefly how I arranged each one. First, you will find each CAP named with a detailed, yet concise, description. I have purposely limited that description to just a few paragraphs. Truth be told, each CAP could take a chapter of its own. But my goal was to provide a quick, yet thorough, introduction and explanation of each one.

Next you will find a self-rating scale to get an approximation on where your present level of implementation might be. The ratings are "weakness", "developing", "capable", "strength", and "command". Each level introduces a slightly more integrative use of the CAP in general practice. It is designed for you to start at the lowest skill level and move up until you find the level that mirrors your implementation. If you lack any one of the indicators in a rating level, then the previous level is your current status.

As you read each one, the nuances might be difficult to distinguish. For example, the description for "strength" might use the word "understand" but the description for "command" might say "use" for the same set of indicators. So, a careful read of each skill level is essential when determining your rating.

Also, choose the skill level that is completely true for you. You might find that a skill level stronger contains some descriptors that are true of you as well but only 1 or 2 that aren't. Use the rating for a starting point that is completely true for you and then begin working on the descriptors in the next level that aren't yet true for you. And of course, be honest. Only then can you improve.

I have included some pointers on how to improve in developing each CAP. The ideas come from my experiences, conversations with fellow administrators and articles that offer advice for improvement or further insight to better understand the skill. What I have provided is just a starting point if you are serious about improvement. Technology today offers a virtual library of information in your home. Research more ways to improve any one of the CAPs as part of your improvement goals. But in order to get you started, any article mentioned or referenced in the CAPs you can find in the final section of the book in Bibliography/References with scores of others that I thought applicable. There is so much good literature out there on the web for you from which to learn and develop. Become an authority yourself on these basic skills and I believe people important to your career and success will notice.

(Note: I use "he, him, she, her and his-or-her" throughout the text. I am in no way trying to suggest there is a difference between effective leadership styles for males or females when using a pronoun in a description. Leadership is leadership.)

KH Meyers

Table of Contents

CAP	Page
Adapting and/or Consolidating	1
Building Capacity in Others	10
Committing to Ethics and Values	19
Considering Others	27
Delegating Jobs and Responsibilities	34
Forming New Ideas	44
Influencing Others	53
Making Decisions	61
Managing/Controlling Performance	68
Monitoring and Managing Interaction	77
Organizing and Planning	88
Motivating Others	96
Presenting Ideas	104
Protecting the Brand	111
Searching for and Selecting Information	118
Seeking Opinions from Others	128
"Take-Charge" Mentality	138
Weighing Multiple Ideas and Concepts	146
Writing for Effect	154
Bibliography/References	160

Adapting and/or Consolidating

Description

Successful leaders are flexible and adaptable. That is, they can change as needed to work effectively within a variety of situations, as well as with different individuals or groups holding varied and often opposing opinions. Leadership requires understanding and appreciating multiple and competing perspectives while tactfully and tactically evaluating ways to consolidate those perspectives or approaches for the good of the company and/or her own position. This skill is most successfully exhibited when the leader adapts or adjusts her approach as the requirements of a situation or problem change. For example, highly skilled and effective use is evident in group discussions or consensus-building dynamics where the leader considers ways to move the group toward her preferred solution to an organizational problem. This kind of strategic flexibility engages logic, consolidation, negotiation, evidence, alliances, compromise and so on. A leader's ability to adapt to emerging conditions or varied opinions and then change her presentation method or strategy to match the flow of the discussion in order to win converts is one of the highest forms of implementation. Analyzing and then offering a solution that consolidates competing ideas often provides a win-win scenario for all the participants in the group. It could also establish her as the most obvious leader during implementation as well.

Leaders lacking in the ability to leverage conditions to match the flow are ultimately marginalized, led by group preferences and overwhelmed by others' situational demands or changes. Competent leaders identify competing factors or forces and then promote that one answer (which could well be a consolidation of various solution options) which best meets the needs of the situation and moves the organization forward. Strong leaders are flexible and effectively adapt and change or consolidate, always thinking of the success of the organization over personal power and prestige.

Self-Evaluation

<u>COMMAND:</u> I to consider multiple and alternate perspectives to my own and even actively seek and question input from relevant sources when making decisions. I openly encourage diverse opinions. I possess a variety of strategies for solving problems, performing job duties, interacting with others, etc. I can provide justification for a selected solution as well as reasons for not selecting other considered solutions and can consistently and seamlessly alter my behavior or approach to effectively respond to situational demands or group dynamics. In group meetings I push for my own solution to be selected but am willing to form alliances with others as long as the core of my solution is intact. I often see the need for organizational change before it is obvious to others or before the problems surface and keep my supervisor informed of possible problems that might affect the work flow or organization structure. The success of the organization above every other consideration is verbalized in my discussions and is always foremost.

STRENGTH: I am clear about the inevitability of change and if needed can identify several alternative solutions from which to pick to meet the new challenges. I can precisely list the pros and cons of each alternative but will remain committed to a chosen solution. Part of my process is to seek feedback from others. I am open to modifications of my original choice if it offers a more complete solution whether it is my solution or another that has more promise of success than mine. The success of the organization is primary to convincing others of my solution. In the group dynamics, I push for my solution to be accepted. However, when the final solution is selected, I am ready for implementation.

CAPABLE: I understand the need for change in my organization and commit to it in order to fit new demands. I can suggest at least one solution to a problem and test it with other members. I weigh the pros and cons of each solution and use some strategies to develop agreement among others in the group toward my choice. I request some input from other members before a final decision but hold to my first-choice solution. In a group situation I advocate my solution, provide reasons and describe the outcome if my solution is accepted. However, I can be swayed from my position.

DEVELOPING: I can pinpoint the failure of the current system to handle a change in the organization but still only limit my involvement and inquiry to a single solution with limited justification for decision and make no attempt to test the solution. I may or may not seek counsel or advice from others and if advice is offered, I give it cursory consideration. In group strategy sessions I may offer a competing solution but have no evidence or reasons for its consideration. Ultimately, I am willing to agree to any solution.

WEAKNESS: Often change happens without me or I may even become irritable as conditions change. I would rather continue with traditional practices in spite of situational demands and altering circumstances. I am very comfortable letting others decide new strategies to resolve a situational conflict. Participating in solutions strategy sessions make me uncomfortable.

Ways to Improve

1. **Tailor your feedback to the experience level of others.** The kind of feedback given toward goal achievement is sometimes governed by the experience level of the other person and whether the feedback is positive or negative. Corrective feedback to an experienced co-worker could increase commitment to the mutual goal because of that employee's understanding of the intricacies of the problem or process. This is especially true the more committed the other person is to meeting the goal. Positive feedback or encouragement, on the other hand, to a novice worker may be the more effective strategy to gain increased goal commitment. A very interesting article written by Jeremy Sutton (2021) provides very practical methods of utilizing feedback with a positive spin.

2. **Understand the nature of groups.** Groups and group members come in all sizes with an infinite number of scenarios. Knowing how to size up a group, a group member, and the direction of a group is imperative in order to navigate through to success. It is important to know how

groups function and utilize that information as you work to harness the ideas and energy of the group. Changing Minds.org (n.d.) provides an excellent resource on how to work within and understand the dynamics of groups. In addition, The South Dakota School of Mines and Technology has published on-line a pamphlet that identifies the elements of an organization that typically influence group proceedings: communication, participation, decision making and organizational roles. It gives very practical advice on how to observe the interactions of the group process.

3. **Are you a Fox, Bloodhound or Donkey?** In a very interesting article titled, *"How to Persuade Different Types of People"*, Martin (2018) explores the group process as it pertains to different personalities and how each personality utilizes a certain behavior toward achieving their desired goal within the group. They are characterized as foxes, bloodhounds and donkeys. The article lays out very solid advice on how to work with each personality in order to understand them and then how move the group forward.

4. **Watch Your Mouth.** Jargon, specialized vocabulary and abbreviated terms turn listeners off if they are unfamiliar with them. In order to persuade others, you need to be sure they are following your presentation. Be thoughtful of terms which can confuse or misdirect others in the group. Identify or define terms as you go along and then check for understanding if they are essential to the position you represent. Smile. Insert needed thinking pauses throughout lengthy presentations.

5. **Learn Your Audience** Here are questions to ask yourself as you prepare for a group meeting that can help: *What do I know about my audience? Who are they, or who do they represent? Are there specific motives for their attendance? What is in it for them? What do they want to get out of being here and how can I best provide it? Are there any overriding concerns they are guarding? What kind of result is needed and how do I get them to move in that direction? What delivery method best matches their aptitude, interests and expectations? That might mean using a technical vocabulary rather than a normal vocabulary, or vice versa. Do I slam on the table to make my*

point or use effective pauses in order to let the information ferment in their thinking? Do I smile and tell jokes or look serious and get right to the point? Understanding your audience helps gear your presentation style to meet the occasion.

Building Capacity in Others

Description

The best leaders support and plan for continuous learning/growth/development for themselves and others using positive and encouraging coaching strategies. Subordinates can count on the leader to provide assistance in learning the skills necessary to be productive and successful. Problems are seen as opportunities to improve through personnel development. Expanding the success and competence of others goes beyond monitoring performance, though that may be and usually is part of the process for improvement. A strong focus on performance improvement involves identifying, assisting, and then monitoring the desired changes and enhancements. Conversations regarding improvement and performance are held regularly and with purpose. Both positive and corrective feedback are important to the process, as is assigning the responsibility for improvement to the employee or subordinate once training or retraining has been completed. Both monitoring the implementation of the new learning and offering specific feedback during the process are essential to lasting change.

The leader also talks about potential for success in one-on-one and group meetings and uses a variety of ways to show approval and note success. The need for building the performance capacity of themselves and their staff is essential and coaching toward successful performance is a regular topic of discussion and planning. (See Organizing and Planning.)

Self-Evaluation

COMMAND: I regularly plan for and take actions directed at developing my own skills as well as those of subordinates. I encourage mid-level managers or leaders to do the same and monitor their success in its application. When needed, I create a written developmental plan that generally follows the SMART (Specific, Measurable, Achievable, Results-oriented and Time-bound) goal-setting improvement model. I look at developmental programs in terms of their potential for sustained improvement. Will they do the job in correcting the problem or develop the necessary skills to make this employee successful with little or no further input or monitoring? I am fully aware which variables (critical attributes) are involved or essential to success when focusing on development like coaching, monitoring implementation and offering both positive and corrective feedback.

STRENGTH: I take responsibility to develop ways and means in order to implement improvement in subordinates or others. Specific steps and plans are designed based on individual needs. Often the plans are written and revised as the needs arise. Inquiry into or evaluation of specific training strategies may take place. I tie development to the organization's vision and performance standards. Monitoring for signs of progress could be more timely and consistent reinforcement could be strengthened.

CAPABLE: When needed, I talk about the need for personal or organizational improvement and identify the specific areas in which development is needed based on hard or anecdotal data. However, I don't develop specific plans to address those needs. I am aware that certain resources may be needed for development, but don't feel it is my job to provide them. I am inconsistent or have not yet developed my own mentoring/coaching skills but know they are important.

DEVELOPING: I understand that developmental needs are important but they are not a constant focus or priority. Honestly, I have no time or background in creating plans for improvement or making suggestions toward improvement but would like to.

WEAKNESS: I show little or no interest in or knowledge of ways to develop others. I might even be seen as ignoring or just plain failing to recognize developmental needs.

Ways to Improve

1. **Mentor/Coach at least 1 subordinate for an entire year.** People new to an organization need specific direction in order to quickly acclimate to their roles and responsibilities. Whether you choose that up-and-coming shining star who will eventually run some part of the company or that person who seems awkward, unsure and out of place (both have their advantages) be sure you understand the commitment and desired outcomes. Mentoring another person for that length of time is a win-win for you both. It not only plants that employee solidly on the road to success but also sharpens your skills to say nothing of the satisfaction derived from watching someone you care about grow and improve. But as it turns out, mentoring goes far beyond that. Effective mentoring requires time, energy, understanding, forgiveness and celebration. Become knowledgeable about the process so both you and the mentee benefit.

Utilize your management team in the same way. Require them to take on at least 1 subordinate to personally mentor for a year. In that situation the person you choose to mentor would be that subordinate manager mentoring him or her on the art and success of coaching and mentoring for the year. Continual personal and effective development lays a solid foundation for training and maintaining an effective organization.

2. **Keep group or organizational goals clear and publicized.** Realistic, understandable goals are critical to the process of development and improvement. If subordinates don't know the critical attributes associated with their job responsibility, expecting them to consistently demonstrate efficiency is unrealistic. If a goal is not clearly defined and actually achievable, employees will have no way to measure their own effectiveness. So, try to make sure employees' assignments are as clear and narrowly focused as possible. Review your expectations regularly in general meetings and in one-on-one conferences. Tie performance reviews to these expectations and be clear on how the ratings or evaluations are connected.

3. **Be a visionary**. In an interesting study by Folkman (2013) he identified 6

characteristics used by effective leaders when inspiring followers. One of the characteristics least correlated was enthusiasm. Good leaders aren't always cheerleaders. One of those more highly correlated with effectiveness is providing a clear vision. Paint the picture of a subordinate's future with you and keep bringing it to the forefront in both formal and casual conversations.

4. **Know your employees.** Rise Staff (2018) wrote, "No one method of leadership and motivation will work for everyone. A good leader understands the diverse styles of their team members and tailors his coaching to each of their unique needs." Observe the mannerisms, likes, dislikes, strengths, weaknesses, commitments, etc. of those under you and use that information to develop a tailor-made approach to help them improve. Some people are strong in the morning and wilt in the afternoon and others just the opposite. Use that knowledge to help them find traction in the organization. Be an observer of your staff, even to the point of taking notes. Don't trust your memory.

5. **Encourage employees to tell their own stories.** Rick (2011) suggests among several other ways to improve employee performance that employees will become more engaged and involved if they are encouraged to tell their own stories. In other words, giving employees the opportunity to tell others—especially peers—a positive incident or the strategy they used to overcome an obstacle to success in their work experience strengthens everyone's belief in the value of the company and of one another. Positive stories build cohesion and loyalty. Personal stories paint in the color and details of the vision and mission statements, and hold deep value. It also gives you a chance to reward that employee for their success and willingness to share with others. [If you haven't read the book, *Lead with a Story* by Smith, (2012) I would suggest you check it out from the local library and see how important personal-organization stories are to supporting improvement.]

Committing to Ethics and Values

Description

Strong leaders maintain a set of values personally and organizationally that guide their interactions with others both inside and outside the organization. Those relationships include peers, subordinates, superiors, clients, community members, and so on. It is a commitment to the stated mission and the purpose of the organization as well as a set of personal standards. The defined values may be limited to the organization, or the leader himself, or a combination of the two, but they cross nearly all aspects of the organization's functions or purpose. Additionally, effective leaders know, point out and easily verbalize the stated and intentional values of the mission. They see those values as a point of reference or mission in communication with others, especially during formal or informal evaluations or developmental opportunities. While a written vision or mission statement isn't essential, strong leaders will not only have them in written form but will display them on communications and in prominent areas of the work place. Values generally have an ethical basis like honesty, care for one another, hard work, assisting others, producing the best product possible, etc. Effective mission/vision statements highlight the essential values and strong leaders are rock solid in adhering to them.

Self-Evaluation

COMMAND: I believe in and have fully internalized the group's work place values. I name them in conversations with others inside and outside the organization and can provide concrete examples of how they are demonstrated in the work place when asked or to make a point of reference. Those beliefs govern my interactions with others as well as determine how I view and carry out my responsibilities daily. I expect others under my influence to know and adhere to the values as well and I constantly monitor employee behavior against the adopted values. I use the formal evaluation process as a means to reinforce, correct or celebrate/reward compliance. I take my own values and ethical behavior very seriously and monitor how well I demonstrate in my own work attitude and responsibilities what I expect of others.

STRENGTH: I take opportunities to promote the group's, company's or organization's values to others including clients, subordinates, peers, supervisors and others. My work manner shows consistent evidence of not just knowing them but having internalized them to the point that I adjust my style to better model the values and, if needed, I regularly remind subordinates that certain behaviors do not reflect the best image on the company or work group in formal or informal discussions. I model my commitment to ethical behavior and work values in the work place.

CAPABLE: I know the group's, organization's or company's values or standards and use them to make decisions within the confines of my own work responsibilities. I discuss them occasionally during interactions with subordinates and particularly if there is a serious breach of ethical conduct reflecting on me or the organization. I am conscious about my own ethical behavior and values and try to be consistent in displaying them in the work place.

DEVELOPING: I can say that I know the company values generally and occasionally use them to govern decisions or interactions. I may focus on a couple of the values when assessing employee competence as a way of making a point with an employee. I have a general set of personal values and ethics that I use for my own work behavior and could name them if asked.

WEAKNESS: I honestly do not know the established values of the company, group or organization or show any measure of commitment to them as a matter of daily work performance. If pressed, I could not name personal governing values of the work place or a set of standards by which I organize my work beliefs.

Ways to Improve

1. **Ask those around you.** In both formal and informal discussions with individuals or small groups ask what they believe the values and norms are for the organization based on what they have observed and experienced. Ask for examples. Write all their observations down. After the meetings, consolidate all the data and share the results. Then as a group or team compare the list with the values or norms stated. Compare them to the mission and vision statements. Celebrate the ones in common and set up some ways to eliminate those values that exist but do not support the company vision and mission. Develop ways to reinforce those states values that are missing altogether from the list.

2. **Revisit the Mission and Vision**. A general rule of thumb is that the mission and vision should be regularly dusted off and re-evaluated to see if they still accurately identify the values and direction of the organization. Utilize representatives of all the company stakeholders to provide feedback and offer changes if an update is called for. Even go so far as to hire someone

from the outside to lead the process to ensure transparency or openness.

3. **Highlight their importance**. In every written and verbal interaction or communication with subordinates and co-workers, reinforce the importance of the values or ethics by which the company or team have agreed to work. Use the language of the value and define it, give examples of it in practice, and encourage employees to relate stories that illustrate it. Make them a part of each and every communication. This is especially important! Be sure you connect them to performance reviews or staff development. Evangelize your staff. Make them believers.

4. **Be sure you live by what you say you believe**. Brainstorm your own core beliefs. Look for evidence of how you hold to them on a consistent basis. Are there examples in your work, conversations, relationships with others, or decision-making that others of the organization can relate to? Identify a feedback team who have the authority and responsibility to report to you individually or collectively examples of when you may have strayed from your core values. Keiling (2021) has listed 83

organizational core values. One way to narrow them down for yourself is to identify your top 15. Then, narrow down those 15 to the top 10 and finally narrow down those 10 to 5. Compare them to the vision or mission. Are they supportive or the organization?

5.**Relate values to promotions**. If you are the person who decides who in the company gets promoted or rewarded in some substantial way, be sure that the recipient, those who might have also been in the running, as well as those who thought they deserved the honor all know how the recipient earned the recognition or promotion based on the company values and standards. Establish a clear path between them. Give examples of what you observed in that employee. Hold up each of the values banners for all to see and make the point that loyalty to the team values, vision, mission is rewarded, looked for and appreciated.

Considering Others

Description

Strong leaders are sensitive to and state the importance of the overall relationship of the organization toward clients, workers, supervisors, community, etc. and implement plans that promote the organization's concern for maintaining that informed relationship. Considering others does not necessarily mean accommodating the ideas or preferences of others inside or outside of the organization, but does mean their needs, concerns, and ideas are measured and even verbalized in the process of determining or changing a policy or procedure, or taking action that might impact those inside and/or outside the organization. Most decisions ripple throughout the organization and beyond. Whomever those ripples reach much be considered and planned for.

A leader does everything possible to manage or promote a positive organizational atmosphere or work climate, as well as market the positive and productive aspects of the organization to the community.

Community image and relationships are serious connections and are always in the framework of a decision. When appropriate, strong leaders involve and inform others in and outside of the organization about relevant information and consider the feelings or impressions of peers, co-workers, supervisors, clients, community. It is important and a matter of practice to keep others informed who are impacted by a decision, action or change. Considerate leaders might ask themselves questions like: *How will this decision affect so-and-so?* Or, *Who needs to be notified or warned about the possible outcomes of this decision?*

Just as importantly, an effective leader works to restrict the flow of negative or hurtful information within or outside the organization and is careful and discerning in written notifications or information that represent herself or the organization. Key to this competency is understanding that actions, decisions, and outcomes affect a variety of groups, organizations and individuals inside and outside the organization.

Self-Evaluation

<u>COMMAND</u>: I make known clearly to others that the actions I take will impact specific groups in and outside the organization and, because of that, I am careful to notify anyone who may be affected by what I do. The possibility of the "ripple effect" that some decisions or actions have is taken into consideration and planned for. I also plan for and undertake the control of destructive or questionable information regarding the organization and work hard to disseminate positive information (especially successes) about the organization. I use marketing strategies to influence how others see or feel about me or the organization. I choose words carefully when addressing others while explaining the impact of a decision.

<u>STRENGTH:</u> I understand clearly and voice openly any concerns that the actions I take will impact specific groups in and outside the organization including other departments within the organization. I consider the influence of the "ripple effect" when making decisions. I believe and share with all concerned that decisions I make will have a positive impact on the work environment or organization.

STRENGTH: I understand any concerns that the actions I take will impact specific groups in and outside the organization including other departments within the organization. I understand the influence of the "ripple effect" when making decisions. I trust that decisions I make will have a positive impact on the work environment or organization.

CAPABLE: I understand and take opportunities to explain how my actions impact specific groups inside the organization.

DEVELOPING: I may make general statements of concern that my decisions will impact others, but I'm not specific as to how the impact might be felt or by whom.

WEAKNESS: I make decisions without regard to their impact of any of the stake holders in or outside the organization

Ways to Improve

1. **Gauge others' perspectives**. "Perspective-taking is about being able to understand a situation from the point of view of another person. The nice thing about this skill is in how it allows us to better explore a situation that happened in the past — or it can support you in making an upcoming decision." (Surdek, 2016).

Perspective-taking is consciously stepping into the shoes of those influenced by a decision and asking questions like: "What do I fear most regarding this decision?" Or, "How will this decision affect my daily routine or practice?" Or, "As an employee does this decision help me or hurt me?" Analyzing the problem or possible solutions from another perspective provides valuable insight into the viewpoints of others.

2. **Map out an "Influence Chart"**. An "Influence Chart" is a simple form that can be used to identify stakeholders that could be touched by a decision. It is as simple as creating columns with the following information for analysis:

- a description of the decision,
- who the stakeholders are,

- who will be touched by that decision,
- how it will influence them, and
- how they will be told or informed.

If there are other considerations that need to be accounted for, they too can be added to the form. Several examples can be searched on-line to review.

3. **Does it influence several ethnicities**? Another consideration is the language of those being affected by the decision. Companies and communities in the United States are multi-linguistic. Surveying the languages within the company and outside in the community could be very important to bear in mind, even to the expense of hiring a certified translator to ensure that the information you are providing is accurate and its intent is properly provided.

4. **Remember change can be hard**. In their blog, "*8 Ways to Communicate Change to Employees*" by Limeade Marketing (2014), steps are provided that will not only soften the blow of a change, but lead toward understanding why the change is necessary. They are simple, direct, comprehensive, and thorough.

5. **Keep up with the new technology**. This is the age of technology and there are several on-line, electronic methods of getting your message out. Stay current on all the ways that people are communicating with one another and use them to your advantage. Web Shop Advisors (2021) has published a very complete article discussing the current media platforms and use. Falling behind this day and age in the information technology sector could be a death nell not only to communicating effectively with your stake holders but to your business's bottom line.

Delegating Jobs and Responsibilities
Description

Leaders at some point hand over responsibility and authority to another person or persons in order to accomplish an organizational goal or solve an organizational problem. That is known as delegation. It could involve any kind of assignment like gathering information, developing a proposal, planning a process, implementing a new procedure, or practically anything. **The delegation must be specific** including a clearly described level of authority (that is, whether the other person can make the final decision or not, or carries with it authority over other employees, schedules, resources etc.). Delegation can also be used when the leader structures HOW the work is to be done in a group or team and divides up different responsibilities to members of the group.

Delegation of authority can range from complete to limited or no authority. What is critical to efficiently and effectively delegating a job or responsibility is that the authority level is clearly enunciated; the required resources are identified, assigned and accounted for, and time lines or deadlines fixed. For example, there is a clear difference between having the authority to develop a plan of action and executing that plan of action. Clarity is of the utmost importance. What are your expectations and what are the limits as you transfer that responsibility over to someone else? It is also important to let others in the organization that might be affected by the assignment know exactly what that person's delegated parameters are. (See Considering Others)

Finally, it is important to remember that delegation is not abdication of responsibility. The supervisor is still responsible for the completion of the task assigned to the subordinate. Failure of the completed task by the subordinate is a failure on the part of the supervisor. Delegation is an excellent tool to be used in developing employee skills (See Building Capacity in Others), though, and can be used as an effective training tool, as well as a way to help reduce the leader's work load. Choosing the right person is essential. When the opportunity is designed more as a teaching experience, just be prepared to step in with new support or direction if the subordinate looks to be floundering so that there is little or no damage to the company or your position.

(NOTE: Assigning a task to an individual that resembles or is similar to the roles or responsibilities already assigned to that individual is not delegation. Delegation is the assignment of a task apart and/or different from that other person's regular duties.)

Self-Evaluation

COMMAND: I am very specific about the task at hand including the history or related factors that might influence success. I also make sure that the person assigned the task knows why he or she was given the assignment. The level of authority and resources available, the time line for completion and finally, the expected standard for successful completion of the task are all outlined and understood. And finally, I inform others in the group or organization of the assignment and the level of authority that person has over them in the process. Touch points are scheduled to check on progress or some form of updates agreed to.

STRENGTH: I am specific when I assign a new task and make sure that person has a clear understanding of the authority that accompanies the task. I also identify which resources are available and in sufficient amount to accomplish the task. I periodically check on progress. I essentially act as a consultant or sounding board but am constantly aware of the actions taken by the person to whom I delegated the role or responsibility.

CAPABLE: I know how to delegate. When I assign a task, I ty to be sure the person has a clear understating of what the task. Sometimes, however, I am not specific about the level of authority or resources needed to successfully complete the task causing some confusion or misunderstanding. Too often, they are not addressed or even mentioned. I tend to forget to check on the progress of implementation. And sometimes I even take back the responsibility even though the subordinate may have things well in hand. At other times I may withhold certain aspects of the needed authority limiting the scope of the assignment.

DEVELOPING: When I delegate a task to someone outside their normal responsibilities, I tend to be general. I am not specific about my expectations or the level of authority that will accomplish the task and often times feel so uncomfortable that I reassume the responsibility. I am not clear on what I expect.

WEAKNESS: I am not comfortable delegating tasks to others. I feel I need to do things myself so that they are done properly.

Ways to Improve

1. **Start small**. DeMers (n.d.) in his article published by INC., *7 Strategies to Delegate Better and Get More Done*, begins with the one suggestion that most business coaches write about when trying to help executives develop delegation skills: let go. In order to delegate there has to be confidence in not only the person you are shifting some of your responsibility over to, but confidence in yourself to choose the right person, the right level of responsibility or authority, the appropriate time line and the expected result as well as make time to monitor along the way. Employees grow and become more valuable as they gain their own sense of confidence by having fulfilled a delegated task. Start small if you need to and see that delegation not only gets things done, but it frees your time to focus on more serious matters. As you move forward, increase the level of and opportunities for delegation.

2. **Use delegation as a way to sharpen your staff's confidence.** Delegation is an effective way to sharpen those employees in whom you see real potential and drive.

Keep a record or file of every employee and note instances of work behavior that indicate certain work characteristics and strengths that can be tapped to reduce your load. Some people are great organizers, others are great communicators. Still others are careful to attend to detail. Delegate tasks that highlight those strengths and watch the employee gain confidence and skill and thus add to the value of the organization. (See Building Capacity)

3. **Celebrate completed tasks.** Continually look for reasons to reward or recognize a delegated job well-done. Be sure to allow time for the employee to tell the story of the delegated task paying particular attention to how he or she successfully maneuvered around or through obstacles. Follow up with your own words of praise and thanks connecting the success, as with any company celebration, with your personal appreciation. (See Motivating Others)

4. **Look for routine tasks you can move off your desk**. Delegation involves any assigned job or responsibility outside the parameters of that person's job description or regular assignment. Leaders are expected to manage the larger picture.

Routine tasks can quietly take up a leader's time and he or she not even be aware of it. Look through your daily tasks. Identify those minor tasks that can be delegated. However, remember that they too have to be carefully considered in all the aspects that go with delegation like, authority, time line, expectations, check-ins and so on. Delegate but stay in control. (Note: Remember, if it is routine practice to hand over assignments to your secretary, then it is no longer delegation. It has become part of the secretary's job expectation. Delegation is the assignment of job or task outside of the person's routine work assignment or role.)

5. **Build in time for learning**. The people to whom you might delegate a task may not have the background knowledge that goes along with experience. That is especially true of someone just exercising some authority or meeting a time line. Build in learning time to every delegated task as appropriate to build the knowledge base of the person chosen. Show patience and understanding as they make mistakes or mishandle their roles. That is all part of the teaching that must happen between you and that employee. Build in time for the

unforeseen training or experience needs of that employee. (See Considering Others)

Forming New Ideas

Description

Developing new ideas is a leadership quality that centers on building a framework, concept or idea from varied sources of information including written, verbal or observational. It is the ability to take multiple bits of information that may even seem unrelated and work them into a single, meaningful concept or hypotheses without regard to when they occurred or their origin. Strong leaders are constantly on the lookout for information and check sources regularly. In fact, they encourage and reward the creative flow of ideas no matter how unusual or "out of the box" so as to use those ideas as spring boards for their own creative thought.

From those bits of information leaders can begin to develop ideas or hunches using a logical process of analysis isolating and explaining which pieces of information led to the conclusions, new ideas or concepts. It is possible that multiple hypotheses may be formed for the same set of informational pieces, but, efficient leaders can also distinguish between major concepts demanding attention or resolution in a timely manner and those which would be considered minor concepts with limited priority or influence. As a result of the new insights, concepts or hypotheses, the leader may set new priorities, new directions, or rewrite policies or procedures.

Leaders also encourage employees to share their ideas and often take time out to brainstorm with collaborative groups a problem or an area of work just to look for solutions. Creative, open minds lead to ideas that lead to new strategies, products and procedures. Strong leaders also make time in their schedules just to think uninterrupted. It is called creating "White Space".

Self-rating Scale

COMMAND: I regularly analyze varied pieces of information in order to develop ideas about the organization. I am constantly assessing the status of the work environment. And as concepts are formed, whether major or minor, I can clearly outline my thinking and the factors which influenced my thinking to others. In group meetings, I find myself looking for links between my ideas and other group members' positions though facts or information at different times may be separated by days, weeks or even months. I hang on to bits of information by either writing them down and filing them away or mentally through key points so as to bring them back as needed. Sometimes I maintain several concepts concurrently addressing the same set of data. Emerging data is mentally or systematically cataloged with the related concepts. Collaboration is an essential method for me to collect new information and create new ideas.

STRENGTH: I am adept at forming major concepts related to work, group or organization and I regularly review information just for that purpose. Sometimes competing concepts are formed to explain the same set of information. Thinking through major and minor concepts is important to me if they influence the success of the organization. Even seemingly unimportant information is viewed and analyzed for connections and relevance. In the group meetings I listen to others' ideas intently in order to offer new links or concepts so as to further the debate or discussion. Thinking of possible outcomes of a particular strategy when agreed upon in the group discussion or dynamics is standard practice for me.

CAPABLE: I form concepts around major factors impacting the group, organization or work place. Generally, I am satisfied if a single concept is formed to explain a set of data. In some group situations, I try to make links from what others say to my ideas or concepts. I tend to hold concepts independent of each other rather than holding them up against one another. I occasionally seek someone else's thoughts.

DEVELOPING: I am able to form concepts about some major items related to my position or function within the organization; however, I may miss some major concepts or ideas because I don't always recognize or allow in important information outside my position. In fact, in group interaction, too often I view ideas or concepts promoted by others in relation to my concept only. I am only interested in how similar they are to my ideas.

WEAKNESS: I don't form concepts or ideas around a construct of information and I tend to make assumptions or conclusions without any supporting data or evidence.

Ways to Improve

`1. **Schedule "white space",** that is unscheduled time. White space is time during the work day that you are free to think creatively. "We need white space in our daily lives just as much as we need it in our designs because the concept carries over: If our lives are over-cluttered and over-booked, we can't focus properly on anything. What's more, this way of working actually shrinks our ability to think creatively" (Glei, 2018). We get lost in our busyness. White space before or after an important meeting can be very productive. It sets you up to be fully "on top of things." Time just to think as a leader is essential to constructing new ideas or concepts.

2. **Think about your mistakes.** Fabrega (2018) in her article, *"How to Learn from Your Mistakes"*, lists several questions to ask after having made a mistake. Rather than wallow in the sense of failure, use that time of reflection as an opportunity for analysis and scrutiny. Not only will it move you forward to avoid the same mistake in the future, but it will also strengthen that

area of the brain designed for creative thought.

3. **Listen for and explore emotion in yourself and others during a dialog.** Ogden (2016) writes about the importance of emotion in the thinking process: "The more I thought about (emotion's connection to thinking), the more I realized that I didn't see emotions and critical thinking as two planets orbiting different suns. In fact, often critically thinking about an issue leads us to have big feelings about the issue. The reverse is true as well. Big feelings often lead us to think critically about an issue. So, feelings and thinking are very connected." If you feel these emotions in yourself, consider which they are and why. If you sense an emotional response in someone else, explore it graciously by asking without condemning or demeaning if they could explain what they are feeling and possibly why. Show interest and resolve to remedy any misunderstanding. That can be very influential in discussion and thus free up the mind to explore ideas. Practice connection with the emotion in yourself and others.

4. Play devil's advocate as often as possible. Purposely take the opposing side to your own stand in an argument or decision. Create as many reasons against your point of view as you have created supporting your point of view. A relatively new term for considering that an opposing view has value is "Intellectual Humility" (Porter& Schumann, 2018). That is, keeping an open mind to the possibility that another view has merit and points of not only interest, but also intersection with your prevailing point of view. After listening to an opposing view in a discussion, ask the other person if you could summarize their thoughts for clarification

5. Create non-sensical mind webs. Such a web creation is more like a mind game that is fun, practical and team-building as well as supporting concept development. Ask your friends, colleagues, spouse, children, etc. to name 3 or more distinct events that could possibly happen in your life, business etc. Then it is your job, or team members' job, to create as many scenarios as possible that would tie all of those events together. For example, I might choose: 1. Boss walks by you without returning your morning greeting, 2. The fire alarm goes off, and 3. Your secretary calls in sick. How could they all be related? This is an entertaining and productive way to begin a meeting to get the creative juices flowing. It also makes for a great ice-breaker helping unfamiliar participants to relax and break down some natural walls.

Influencing Others

Description

Good leaders need to be convincing when they communicate their ideas whether during a one-on-one conference or in a group setting. And they do so by using techniques successfully that move or influence others toward adoption of their own position(s). One of the ways it is accomplished is by verbal interaction. Being direct, for example, tends to establish credibility. Another way is by modeling or behaving in the way the leader wishes the others in the group would adopt. Yet another is to be assertive but not aggressive. Still and another is to tie himself or his position to the power, reputation, goals and aims of the organization or work group including using his or her own status or position. In any case, he works to be sure his own ideas are clear and that others are attentive to his presentation. While an effective leader may not ultimately move the individual or group to his position, he is nonetheless skilled at using all the necessary and effective measures to present himself well. Others in the group know well what the leader's position on the issue is and why. Leaders demonstrating a consistent style of flexibility and trustworthiness carry most employees through change and progress.

Self-rating Scale

COMMAND: When I take a position on an issue, I tie my rationale to the values and beliefs that support the high standards and reputation of the organization or work group. During group meetings or brainstorming, and especially in planning sessions, I listen carefully so I can capitalize on the similarities and interests of positions proposed by others so as to show how my position accommodates their main points. I might also connect my position with those of the supervisor, goals of the organization, or welfare of the group and make those connections clear during the give-and-take of the group. I use language which helps the group visualize the positive or reasonable outcomes of adopting my position. I value flexibility and trustworthiness and treat others that way.

STRENGTH: I use proven techniques to influence others in the group to adopt my ideas; for example, I use information efficiently as the basis for justifying or adopting my position. I listen attentively so that I can find opportunities to tie the components and interests of my ideas to those of others in the group discussion thus strengthening my own position.

CAPABLE: In group meetings I hold the attention of others when presenting and use techniques that allow for a clear understanding of my position and rationale. I use available information effectively and press for understanding of the others toward my position by asking questions of group members. If the interaction is with an individual, I ask for response for clarity of what I am saying. I am known to express some concern over having my ideas accepted or adopted but am not always convincing when I do so.

DEVELOPING: I can hold the attention of others in the group during presentation but not well or convincingly and often lose the support of the group toward my ideas. I don't often offer information in a convincing way.

WEAKNESS: I really don't show any urgency or desire in group situations such that I bring others around to my position on an issue. In fact, I just don't have the communication skills necessary to sustain the attention of others in my presentation.

Ways to Improve

1. Your language is a dead giveaway. Others tend to listen and follow a person who uses language of certainty and confidence. Words like "might", "maybe" or "attempt" leave the listeners with questions and uncertainty. Language like "will", "must" or "can" establish a sense of confidence and future. Convincing others through body language (smile, straight posture, open arms, and firm handshake) and language help to line others up behind you.

2. Know what you are talking about. There is no substitute for having a thorough knowledge about the issue under discussion. If there is time to investigate, collect data, and interview those a new decision or policy will affect, it is time well spent. Deconstructing a problem into its respective parts gives you the advantage in discussions and establishes a solid foundation from which to take a leadership position. Part of the investigation or fact finding should involve information and agenda of those you are trying to convince. Sometimes it is not enough to know the problem. You might gain even more leverage knowing the hidden schemas that are being held by others at the table.

3. Make critical connections. There are usually several sides to consider when dealing with a problem affecting others within the organization. Taking the position that will support the core principles, mission and messaging of the organization establishes credibility to an argument. Outlining the connection your side has with those core principles is much more influential than trying to establish a new way of thinking or, even worse, one that contradicts those basic principles. In the same way, establishing that a different position is in opposition to those core principles makes for a strong position from which to build acceptance.

4. Be Prepared with a Plan. Loehr (2018) reviews a 6-step process known as the Cohen-Bradford Influence Model for a person without authority in a position of having to influence someone else. Those steps are:

- Assume That Everyone Can Help. Keep in mind that trust is an important commodity. Believe in the good nature of people until they prove themselves otherwise.

- Establish your Objectives. "You have to stay focused and remember the very reason why you want to influence these people. What is the benefit of having these people on your side? What is your ultimate goal?" From the beginning let everyone in on your set of priorities.
- Understand the Other Person's Situation. Listening attentively with the intent to understand is imperative. Clarify the other person's stance through questions and restatements. Be sure you understand what concerns and facts they are bringing to the table and discussions. People who feel understood are much more likely to return the same courtesy.
- Identify What Matters, to You and to Them. "If you take your time hearing the other person, you will understand exactly what is truly important to them; knowing what he or she values most is likely to be the determining factor in this model."

- Analyze the Relationship. Question the strength and limits of your relationship. Has it been a long-standing friendship? Is this a newly established relationship? Are there any common bonds? How much influence do I have already?
- Make the "Exchange". In every negotiation both sides need to bring to the table any exchange currency that might help make the bargain. What do you have in your arsenal that you can trade for what you are wanting from his? Concessions move everyone involved closer to the goal. Be sure you are clear about your "can't-do's". Ultimately the goal is to find a combination of agreements that will lead to the exchange.

5. **Connect your thoughts to their thoughts**: One of the most effective techniques in influencing others is to present your ideas within the framework of their own concerns or ideas. Looking for and/or creating connections and building your position from that foundation mitigates as least some of the opposition.

Making Decisions

Description

Strong leaders with an internal need toward being decisive are always ready, willing and able to make decisions and stick with them. They display a strong sense of confidence in their decisions and plans to move forward even in the face of obstacles or opposition. Once a decision is made, the leader's emotional and mental readiness prepares her to take charge, develop a plan of action, deliver a judgment, take necessary actions and commit herself and others. Strong leaders do so regardless of the quality of the decisions or actions. (See Organizing and Planning.)

The quality of decisiveness is not related to the outcome of a decision. The results of the decision might turn out to be catastrophic. Internally and outwardly a decisive leader holds firmly to the notion that the goals or objectives will be successfully achieved and is always ready to make the decision when requested or naturally part of their responsibilities. (General

Custer was decisive and self-confident, for example.)

Decisive leaders show little-to-no hesitation or ambivalence. They relish being the quarterback on the field. Decisive leaders can provide their rationale or the information considered if questioned by others, believe in themselves and their capability, and provide clarity to a process when called upon.

Being decisive is different from acting proactively. The latter is seeing something that needs to get done and taking charge to get it accomplished. Decisiveness is about the internal preparedness, mindset and the willingness to decide and then displaying unshakable confidence in that decision. It is the preparedness mentally to make a decision as opposed to actually carrying out the decision itself. (See Take-Charge Mentality)

Self-rating Scale

<u>COMMAND:</u> I am clear that all major decisions will come from me. Some minor decisions may be referred to subordinates. I explain to subordinates how I arrived at my decision and why the decision will work. My mannerism always displays my confidence in my decisions. I often compare my decisions with alternative possibilities and outline why my final decision is superior to the others. While I make most decisions by considering all available data, sometimes my decisions are made at the gut level or based solely on my previous experiences; they might be called "intuitive".

<u>STRENGTH:</u> I assume responsibility for all major decisions facing the organization in my assigned role. I will delegate some decisions for lesser problems to subordinates. Once the decision is made, I take opportunities to explain why and how I reached the decision. Considering alternative points of view is part of the decision-making process for me. Once I have made a decision, I am confident it will succeed.

<u>CAPABLE:</u> When needed, I can and do make decisions on any major decisions facing the organization. As I feel it appropriate, I will consider alternative points of view before the decision is made but pretty much hold on to the responsibility of the final decision. I can explain my rationale if required, but "hope" internally it was the right decision.

DEVELOPING: I can make a decision when required or the circumstances demand it. Often, though, the decisions are ambiguous and justifications aren't supported with data. Sometimes if I sense the need for a decision involves a minor issue, I let events work out a solution. Sometimes I even let subordinates manage it.

WEAKNESS: I struggle to make a decision when the opportunity presents itself. Or, when I do make a decision it is often confusing or ambiguous to others, and I can't offer much, if any, rationale.

Ways to Improve

1. **Video Games can help.** Online Business writes for *Manpower* (2010) that one of the more interesting ways to improve decisiveness is to play video games requiring rapid movements and immediate decisions. This is supported by research done years ago. Fast response games improve decisiveness and hand-eye coordination, for example, as well as multitasking. So, pick your favorite video game, challenge the kids and enjoy the game while you are sharpening your skills.

2. **Preparing others is critical**. Folkman (2013) relays 4 steps to follow in order to make decisions with purpose and increased success. He reminds the reader that while gathering good data and facts are important to the process of making a decision, the human element cannot be ignored. Inspiring people is an important part of the process. Painting for others how the decision will improve their conditions or solve a problem is just as important as the decision itself. Preparing people mentally and emotionally are critical to the advent of the decision.

3. **Request opportunities from those above you**. Ask your manager for opportunities to make decisions for existing problems along with time to meet throughout the process for that manager's feedback and corrective action if needed. Even the seemingly smallest of decisions requires attention to detail, a plan of action and follow through. When your manager sees that you have a process in place, are careful to find and review pending data or facts, and conclude with a reasonable, workable solution, the more likely opportunities will come your way. Be content to start small and work your way up to more important decisions as you gain experience.

4. **Practice with established time constraints**. Young (2007) suggests to readers that they time their decisions. Deciding on where to go out to eat, for example, should take no more than a few seconds to a minute. Major decisions no longer than 5 minutes even if that decision is to do more fact-gathering. As soon as a problem is presented, start the stop watch.

5. **List your successes.** Ryan (n.d.) suggests a very simple method of building up your self-confidence: First, write down

all of your strengths, even the smallest or less noticeable. Second, list all of your successes you can think of. Use those lists as a daily reminder of your capabilities. Read them. Refer to them. Add to the lists as you continue to add to your successes and identify new strengths.

Managing or Controlling Performance

Description

Competent leaders create and use effective methods to provide feedback on performance, delegated assignments or work accomplished by self and others within their scope of authority. The type of feedback can vary between subjective/observational to objective/data-driven. These plans and methods to measure performance of peers, subordinates, delegated jobs, etc. are often set against accepted standards, including past performance measurements.

Good management control also means designing and scheduling checkpoints used to accurately monitor progress or provide targeted feedback about performance of all parties involved in the process. Clear and concise feedback is provided to employees when their work is not meeting the accepted or expected standards including new performance goals and methods outlined on how to meet those goals.

Performance feedback is fair, honest and firm, never personal.

Self-rating Scale

<u>COMMAND</u>: I set and measure performance standards or assignments. In doing so, I establish a time for a checkpoint to review progress and have already established a contingency plan if standards aren't met. (For example: "If our customer rating does not equal or exceed 85% 'good' or 'very good' on the surveys, then we will try____") When delegating tasks, I want and ask for specific feedback on completion progress of task or results. I set up a time line for reviews when a new process or procedure is introduced and check the progress against the established standard. I am good at praising those who consistently model work-related behavior reflecting expected standards. I am, however, careful to discuss unacceptable work-related behavior of subordinates privately by reviewing the expected standard, developing an improvement plan with the employee that outlines specific measurements of acceptable performance and setting a time for follow-up review.

<u>STRENGTH</u>: I design outcomes with specific criteria or standards as a guide to measure progress. When delegating, I want reports of feedback on results or actions assigned at a specific time in the future. Feedback or review meetings are held with established standards as the agenda. I review work behavior constantly to ensure that it meets or exceeds work standards. If it does not, I privately review substandard performance with subordinates and set up expectations for improvement.

CAPABLE: I request feedback or measurement of outcomes associated with actions or jobs of the organization, but I often leave out a comparison of that feedback with a set of standards. In fact, measurable standards may or may not exist. I like to publicly praise work behavior that meets expected standards, but too often I publicly review work behavior that is not meeting the expected standard in a group setting. I do not hold specific employees accountable for not meeting their share of the standard.

DEVELOPING: I monitor performance and understand and sometimes state the need for a follow-up in conversations with subordinates when suggestions are made for improvement, but do not follow through with scheduling a time for it. I can be unclear as to the specific measures that will be reviewed. I do notice when subordinate behavior or work is "up to standard" though and may comment on it.

WEAKNESS: Honestly, I have little or no sense of how to set up a way to effectively and meaningfully measure performance—mine or anyone else's. And when I do talk with a subordinate about poor performance, follow-up isn't scheduled to ensure compliance.

Ways to Improve

1. **Self-Improvement is the key**. Improving your own performance is the first step toward understanding how to improve someone else's performance. Identify specifically the standards of production, behavior, or characteristics that are the core to your and/or your company's identity. Determine the ways in which you demonstrate those factors and determine at the beginning of each week; how are they evident in your job responsibilities? Verbally lay out your schedule and talk your way through it and the points when your performance will be the most visible and critical, Then, at the end of the week take time to evaluate your performance. Be critical! Were there any indicators that lead you to believe you hit the mark or were a total miss? Look for indicators like feedback from subordinates or supervisor, missed production targets, and so on. Be observant; collect any data relevant to your performance. When you understand and identify fully with your core principles, and model them for your subordinates, you can

then hold others accountable to those standards.

2. **Use a variety of methods when working on others' improvement**. For employees who continue to perform at a high level, your feedback isn't always challenging enough to keep them motivated. The on-line performance assessment company, Testofy (May 2016), lists 5 of the most effect employee performance evaluation methods: Critical Incident, 360 Evaluation, Checklist Method, Performance Test Method and Self-Evaluation Method. Try letting workers set their own performance goals—always based on the core standards—as well as design the method of measurement. Just be careful to monitor their goal. Does it stretch them or is it an opportunity to skate for a while? You may already have some data that shows their current production level so that the challenge for them in setting their own goal is how to go even further or faster. Bring the data to the meeting and ask for their interpretation or synapses. Get you employee involved in his own review.

3. **Continuously monitor morale**. When a team, department, company is

constantly scrutinized and devalued, morale suffers and production will always decline. Good managers and leaders are always testing the climate to gauge the feelings and limits of those working. Morale is stronger when employees know what is expected, those expectations are fairly and reasonable applied and those meeting and exceeding expectations or standards are recognized and rewarded.

4. **Know your team members**. Berglas (2013) presents an excellent perspective on the five types of resistant employees: Gorillas, Foxes, Owls, Skunks and Equidae (Horses) and how to work with each one. Every leader runs across those subordinates who refuse to get on the change train. They cry, cajole, threaten and run in hopes of being left behind. It is very important that these employees especially are helped through the process of change or allowed (encouraged) to find a new occupation.

5. **Counseling a resistant employee may provide a path toward improvement**. In a very informative look at counseling resistant people, Shallcross (2010) reviews some very specific ways originated by Robert Wubbolding, Director of Training

for the William Glasser Institute and Director of the Center for Reality Therapy in Cincinnati, to help move a resistant client toward acceptance or at least understanding. The techniques described could easily be used in a conference or a performance review to overcome resistance to change by a subordinate. Often times employees are resistant or underperforming for a reason yet to be disclosed. By setting aside the immediate problem of performance but seeking to understand the underlying personal issue through counseling may lead to not only salvaging an employee, but resolving the performance issue. When those problems have been worked through, it could then allow for the work-performance discussion to continue with positive results.

Monitoring and Managing Interaction
Description

There are times when leaders have to manage the interaction between others. When dealing with interaction of others the leader monitors, controls and evaluates the methods, frequency and health of a group's or organization's communication whether written or verbal. Because of the leader's belief in the importance of communication and full involvement with the organization, he devises ways to provide positive, constructive opportunities for all subordinates to express their concerns as well as their appreciation with the goal that it will encourage a feeling of inclusion. Sometimes the supervisor makes decisions as to the grouping of personnel in work-group assignments considering communication styles of those involved as a factor. Also, team leaders use effective processes to keep the conversation or communication positive and moving toward the goal. Skills like intervening, negotiating, or conflict resolution are employed as needed in the group discussions in order to facilitate communication and create a cooperative atmosphere. Monitoring the communication process includes stopping damaging, accusatory or irrelevant conversation that limit or subvert the group's progress toward a desired end. When needed, a strong leader mediates when there are diverging or conflicting opinions or positions. Leaders use any of the following skills as a group facilitator effectively: modeling, summarizing, noting progress, redirecting conversation, encouraging inclusion and employing silence.

Self-rating Scale

<u>COMMAND</u>: I develop and implement ways to legitimize the relationship between self and other(s) comprising a "team" while at the same time take actions that solidifies my position as the leader. For example, I call meetings and choose the participants. The language of "us", "our", or "we" is a primary expression in discussions in most conversations even in evaluation conferences. A climate of togetherness and team are regularly evaluated and adjusted as needed. I often take on the responsibility of initiating team processes like setting up sub-teams or working groups in order to move the whole team toward goal accomplishment. I identify common threads, thoughts or concerns for the group to consider. I take responsibility for keeping the communication lines open, clear and functioning and work to get all participants involved in the discussion by tracking participation and targeting those who had not given voice to their opinions. I try to handle personnel or organizational obstacles in a decisive manner in order to keep clear the lines for positive communication and look for opportunities to work alongside of subordinates.

STRENGTH: I create opportunities for meetings or communications to take place in the work environment as they are needed and work to ensure that all involved have contributed to the meeting. During group discussions, I look for similar thoughts or concerns in order to build consensus among the group. I am just as likely to enter into unscheduled or casual communication opportunities emphasizing the need for understanding amongst all the stake holders. I regularly query employees' feelings to be sure they are comfortable communicating during personal conferences (evaluations, for example) or organizational reviews. I mediate differences in positive ways by identifying similarities and mutual benefits and change facilitator strategies as needed.

CAPABLE: I state the need for and importance of collaboration and cooperation. I am not as good at monitoring the work place climate for signs of health with regard to employee comfort but am able to get everyone to participate to some level. I use open-ended questions like, "Does anyone have any suggestions about..."? Feedback and understanding in one-on-one conferences are a priority.

DEVELOPING: I am aware that others have ideas and that their contributions have value but often use their thoughts only with regard to how they relate to my own position. While I want everyone to participate in the communication process or work together, I don't always work or plan for that to take place. I am known for presenting my own ideas to the group primarily to influence the group for my purposes. Contribution reveals a singular focus on own ideas and outcomes. I don't use facilitation strategies regularly or effectively.

WEAKNESS: I admit I throttle opportunities for group communication; additionally, in a group situation I state my position on a problem or organizational issue and behave in ways which will solely implement my position. I might resort to communication strategies like arguing, limited problem-solving, persuasion or unilateral decision making. I may even step aside and allow group conversation and interaction to move with no direction or purpose. I am unaware of how to use collaboration, agreement, or consensus or any other facilitator role and skills.

Ways to Improve

1. **Understand the communication process**. Kay (2016) writes about 4 different communication styles present in a group. Successful leaders need to be able to identify, understand and work with each of the styles. She identifies those styles as either fast or slow-paced combined with either people-oriented or task-oriented. In other words, a person can be fast-paced and people-oriented, or fast-paced and task-oriented. They can be slow-paced and people-oriented or slow-paced and task-oriented. In the group communication process, or even one-on-one, the key is to listen, analyze their style of communication and then utilize the same style so as to effectively communicate. She also presents typical phrases used for each of the styles along with some of the most common mistakes that communicators make when trying to be heard.

2. **What to do about electronic communication**. In an article published by Find Law (n.d.), some very practical guidelines for any employer or supervisor to consider before making a mistake trying to

monitor the digital communication of employees are offered. They are:

- Establish a Policy: Don't let there be any confusion about whether a particular form of communication will be monitored or not. Create a clear policy that outlines what forms of communications are monitored, why they are monitored and under what circumstances they are monitored. To be extra careful, consider having employees sign a consent form acknowledging that they understand and agree that their workplace communications will be monitored.

- Have a Justification for Monitoring: Courts are far less likely to find you liable for violating an employee's right to privacy if you have a good, work-related reason for monitoring communications. If you've had past experiences that prompted monitoring or have received complaints, these all qualify as perfectly good justifications for monitoring employee communications.

- Be Reasonable: Be smart about how and when you monitor employee communications. If you create a draconian atmosphere of surveillance or implement a system that seems excessive given the potential problems, a court is much more likely to find that you are violating employee privacy rights. Ensure that your monitoring system is proportional to any potential problems because overreaching is a good way to ensure a lawsuit from a disgruntled employee.

3. **Get feedback about your own performance**. Another way to lay the groundwork for establishing a clear communication channel is to ask for feedback on your own performance. Statements to others like: "I would really like to know how you see my performance as your supervisor (colleague, peer, etc.) because I want to continue to improve. Is there anything you can share with me that I could do differently that would make your job easier and my performance more effective?" Those kinds of statements honestly asked over time will yield positive bonds with others in the organization and open opportunities for self-growth. Feedback at first might be minimal or cautionary, but with evidence of listening and changing, more substantial feedback will follow.

4. **A feedback technique**. At your next group meeting try a feedback technique called "Thumbs Up. Thumbs Down". At the conclusion of the meeting go around the group and ask each person to give a "thumbs up" indicating a positive outcome of the meeting for them or a "thumbs down" indicating a negative or unexpected point from the meeting. They can then expand on their choice without fear of retribution or challenge from any other members of the group.

5. **Encourage positive interactions**. Watson (2010) begins her article outlining 10 ways to improve the communication model in a business or group by reminding the readers that good communication is a matter of establishing a culture of communication in the organization. Further, she shares that an "open door" policy goes a long way in neutralizing negative communication before it can build beyond repair. Use a diplomatic approach (nonjudgmental and open minded). Carefully listen to the spoken and unspoken words. Monitor the body language and read between the lines. Inviting information from all sides is essential. She continues by commenting on

importance of considering cultural differences and maintaining trust. All of these techniques form a healthy climate in which everyone feels safe to share their thoughts and concerns.

Organizing and Planning

Description

Organization and planning are demonstrated when a leader shows an awareness that there are components, schedules, actions and plans needed in order to implement or complete an assignment, program, process or task for which he or she is immediately or ultimately responsible. The skills to organize and plan a one-hour meeting are the same as those for a multi-month application project often requiring extensive collaboration. Leaders talented in this attribute think beyond the immediate or obvious and plan for and determine how the assignment, task etc. will impact personnel and/or resources including time, for example. Little to nothing is left to chance.

The overall goal is to effectively utilize personnel, materials, resources and time so that delays are mitigated or even avoided. It is forethought planning to a large degree. Effectively prioritizing steps and utilizing schedules is key to success. Agendas are completed and shared with those affected. A strong leader thinks through possible risks and plans for alternate paths to reach the goal. There are generally Plans B and C in the wings to account for unforeseen or mitigating circumstances.

Planning also involves monitoring subordinates to make sure everyone involved is on the "same page". The oversight of personnel connected with any project, large or small, is accounted for and those being responsible are notified on how the oversight will take place. These skills are often accompanied by To-do lists, Running lists, Calendar planners, time lines and so on.

Effective planning and organizing very often are accompanied by several of the other CAPs skills like Delegation, Management of Interaction, Taking Responsibility and Decision-making. Analysis, focus, prioritization and attention to detail further support effective planning.

Self-rating Scale

COMMAND: I establish clear, detailed schedules outlining tasks, time lines, priorities, resources and responsibilities assigned to specific individuals. I plan for both the major and minor components. When needed, I hold meetings or communicate in other ways (memos, emails, one-on-one conversations, etc.) the schedule and related information to subordinates. Everyone touched by the plan is informed and included. I communicate the necessary information regarding agendas and times for called meetings ahead of time. Allocation of resources is completed and contingency plans are thought out and ready if needed. I maintain a number of personal methods to help with planning and organizing.

STRENGTH: I can establish a well-planned, detailed schedule for implementing the major components of the process, procedure or task. Priorities indicating assigned importance have been established and subordinates have been informed of involvement and schedule. Coordination of various components or groups is given consideration and accounted for as I share the plan with others. I keep a running calendar, To-do list or some other physical method of tracking plans and progress.

CAPABLE: I am known for establishing a well-planned, schedule of immediate and future events for implementing the major components of any process, procedure or task. And I work to complete the basic expectations or requirements of the planning stage. Sometimes the minor components of any plan like personnel or timelines are lost or marginalized in my planning.

DEVELOPING: I show limited organizational ability by suggesting the need for planning meetings. I sometimes show concern about the need to revisit or attend to current or past problems but do not put a plan in place to do so, or the plan is woefully incomplete.

WEAKNESS: Inadequate attention is given to planning. Schedules and priorities are nonexistent or incomplete. High priority demands are missed or left unattended.

Ways to Improve

1. **Identify the Outcome**. In his article, "*Everyday Management: Tips for Busy Leaders*" (2016), Price writes about the importance of identifying and preparing for success by asking 3 key questions about the end result expected of you in your position. First, identify your role and the key outcomes that would reflect a superior performance in that role. Then, answer these questions: 1. How can I measure these key results? 2. What activities are necessary in order for me to achieve these key results? 3. What new or improved skills will help me achieve these key results? These questions work in any capacity of leadership or position from manager to mailroom. When you organize your thinking and target the behavior which will result in superior performance then the only possible outcome is success. Plan to succeed.

2. **Explore To-do Lists**. Using "To-do" lists is one of the most effective and popular ways to organize your time. Carniol (2018) lists 3 ways to manage your lists: First, list everything you want or need to accomplish at the beginning of each work period.

Second, prioritize the list from most to least important. Once the activities or goals are prioritized, rewrite them from most to least important. The author even suggests highlighting important goals in order to keep them in the forefront.

Carniol also suggests that you post the list where you will see it throughout the day. Too often "to-do" lists are written and then buried beneath the "immediate" needs of the day.

One other suggestion is to notify those who might be connected to your 'to-do" that you will be focused on completing a certain task and may need their input or help.

3. **Look for commonalities**. Sometimes there are commonalities inherent in tasks that will allow you to kill several birds with one stone. Looking for those commonalities may save time in the long run. For example, if one task requires a visit on another floor working with a colleague and different task can be handled on the same floor with a different colleague, combine them. Look for threads that link tasks in ways that will make it easier for you to utilize your time or other resources efficiently.

4. **Begin delegating.** One of the other basic skills outlined in the 19 CAPs is Delegating. Delegating can be the most useful tool in planning and organizing. For large projects either in complexity or length in time, dividing up the responsibility among others can be a very useful plan in and of itself. Of course, with delegation comes monitoring the progress of each one of the subtasks by meeting with those you have handled over that portion of the project. In fact, anytime you are reviewing your "to-do" list you should be looking for tasks that can be handed off to others, usually subordinates. Delegation is another way of organizing your resources.

5. **Mind map obstacles**. Practice creating possible obstacles to the completion of a task. There are always road blocks, detours and dead batteries in life and that is just as true for tasks that are your responsibility. Practice preparing for any detours or obstacles by thinking up as many as possible. Write them down, identify the factors that may be the reasons for that problem and finally list your plan to both avoid and or minimize their influence. Not only is this a challenging exercise, but is a great

management skill. Before long, it becomes a natural part of the planning process. Obviously, no one person can anticipate every possible dead end, but with enough practice an effective, seasoned leader will automatically select the most likely challenges to completing his tasks or goals and how to overcome them.

Motivating Others

Description

Effective leaders focus on goal attainment and what is needed to reach those goals including the often-difficult task of motivating others. He sets high internal work standards and goals while regularly reminding staff or subordinates about the importance and purpose for meeting those standards. The possibility of exceeding the standards and setting even higher ones is often discussed or promoted, even planned for and celebrated individually and corporately. Quality control, efficient use of time and resources are all seen as components of achievement. Strong leaders seek and arrange for feedback on progress toward meeting those goals in measurable, quantitative ways which are routinely shared with the staff or subordinates and for which they are held accountable. The supervisor's own personal professional goals are challenging yet reachable. Events or personnel that prevent achievement are personal causes of frustration; they are noted as failures and their effects are taken personally. Strong leaders inform others of their failures for the purpose of improvement.

Praise, when offered, should be meaningful and heart-felt, often mentioning the obstacles overcome to reach the standard. Carefully constructed praise often includes what the future looks like because the standards are met. Celebrations are often planned and carried out as a surprise to say, "Thank you".

Self-rating Scale

COMMAND: I keep others informed and focused on achieving personal or group goals using multiple ways including: personal conferences, group assessments or brainstorming. The goals are challenging, yet reachable. Specific plans, which include the methods, personnel, time lines and resources to reach the goals are in place and a process for measuring success includes demonstrable comparisons with past performances. Data collection is ongoing. Plans include contingencies to overcome barriers or resistance. Descriptions or discussions of how meeting the standards will improve the overall work environment in various ways are common—for example: increasing efficiency, improving group productivity and boosting morale.

STRENGTH: I have established specific goals to improve performance of others or of the group for various areas of responsibility. Detailed plans including personnel, time, resources and acceptable quality are developed to meet those goals. Data from past is used to measure current levels of attainment or setting future goal levels. I often mention obstacles that were set aside to reach the goal. My praise is heartfelt and the accolades sincere.

CAPABLE: I set one or more measurable, challenging goals for improvement with regard to work, task or problem. I don't identify the details or comparisons at the same time. I am aware and discuss occasionally past performance measurements. I challenge peers and/or subordinates that when we accomplish group or individual goals morale improves and we all do better.

DEVELOPING: Occasionally I make statements about the "need to improve", but I don't have any specific standards or goals in mind or mention to subordinates. I don't talk with others about how the present level compares to past performance levels. I do believe achievement is related to morale.

WEAKNESS: I don't show any concern for setting or achieving challenging organizational goals or priorities in performance of self or others. I may hold a mental idea of what needs to be accomplished and will gladly share them when asked

Ways to Improve

1. **Lay out clear expectations**. People are much more motivated when they clearly understand what is expected. Part of that understanding is describing what success and failure each look like to you, along with the rewards and consequences. Personal performance reviews—scheduled and unscheduled—are the proper format to clarify and emphasize those expectations. During these conversations the company's goals and mission are held in the forefront and highlighted as "why" that person's performance is critical to the company's success. To ensure that important points are covered, take the time to outline them before hand, check them off during the conversation as they are discussed, and provide a copy for the employee. Clear, measurable expectations are the basics for employee performance and motivation.

2. **Praise is important**. Recognition using praise, encouragement and positive feedback moves people toward success much more effectively than correction. Not only are these positive comments offered to the employee in specific terms, but they are

highlighted once again when the employee is complimented publicly. All of us want to feel special and managers should capitalize on every opportunity to tap into that emotional need. In his article, DeMaio (2009) shares very effective advice on how to offer praise effectively.

3. **Consider coaching.** Coaching techniques are another way to move people toward personal success. Heathfield (2018) outlines steps that can be used to coach an employee toward stronger performance:

- Focus on the unacceptable behavior not on the employee. Describe your observations as they apply to that behavior.
- Identify any mitigating factors which may be road blocks toward meeting the needed expectations like training, equipment, prevailing attitude or some other factor. Together decide how that obstacle will be removed.
- Identify what success looks like and begin to outline the steps needed to reach that goal. Ask the employee for suggestions as the steps are developed.
- Write out the plan along with the expected behavioral outcomes and the

responsibilities for anyone involved in the improvement—including yourself. Each expectation should have a set of plans that both agree will lead to improvement.

- Set a date and time to check on progress.
- Finish the coaching conference by offering positive encouragement and expressing your sincere belief that the employee does have the capacity to improve.

5. **Concern is a motivator**. Care and concern may be the most underutilized techniques for improving performance there are. People, all people, have a desire to be understood, cared about and believed in. The time managers put into knowing each employee's particular way of accepting praise or a need for improvement cannot be over-emphasized. Some like the pat on the back, others an off-handed comment in person. Some love to get that note of thanks in their locker. Supervisors who come along side an employee struggling with personal issues will reap a life time of gratitude and loyalty. The personal touch means

finding ways to "touch" that employee in a very personal way.

Presenting Ideas

Description

Leaders are regularly expected to make presentations to others formally and informally, planned and spontaneous. Strong leaders must be able to clearly, succinctly and sometimes forcefully present their opinions or ideas. When doing so, effective leaders are prepared with the right information and/or data and adept at using supportive technical, visual, electronic and graphic aids. Preferably, the presentation is rehearsed and thought out well before hand. Within the presentation, opportunities are given for listeners or participants to ask questions.

In addition to formal group presentations, strong leaders are able to effectively communicate their ideas and thoughts in one-on-one conferences. While the object is not to demand conformity by others, it is to convince others of her position and garner acceptance and support. Body language, voice tone and volume, simplicity, and framing the story correctly are all techniques strong presenters attend to.

Self-rating Scale

COMMAND: I am confident presenting my positions or opinions to others whether in a group or to individuals and can present them in very convincing ways. I am current on all the technical and electronic means available for making formal presentations and use them selectively and prepare any needed visuals well ahead of time. I am careful to allow for questions so as to minimize any misunderstandings. I even practice my formal presentations ahead of time being cognizant of my word choices and ways to make important points "stick out". I make sure my major points are presented in a number of ways and am careful to project confidence through my voice, body language and story frame.

STRENGTH: I enjoy making presentations and can generally win over people to my position. I have some tried-and-true methods of presenting that I stick to that have been effective in the past but am familiar with a couple of the more current electronic mediums. Questions are important and I try to make time for them. I try to check to see that my major points were received. I am comfortable using technology to enhance my presentation.

CAPABLE: I spend time getting ready for a presentation but am always a little uncomfortable when actually presenting. I know my major points and focus on making sure I get those across. My presentations are clear and I use language that resembles the group to whom I am addressing. I can prepare and use basic technology techniques.

DEVELOPING: I take minimal steps to prepare for a presentation and am nervous that my ideas will not be understood or accepted. I don't like questions because I am unsure that I can answer them. I can use a dry-erase board or prepare an image or graph as a visual aid, but not much more.

WEAKNESS: I panic at the thought of making a presentation in front of people. I know when I do present my major points are lost in my presentation. I tend to shut down questions. I just am too afraid I won't know the answer.

Ways to Improve

1. Be aware of your comfort level. In his online article, "20 Ways to Improve Your Speaking Skills", Kim (2018) lists a number of ways to improve a presenter's comfort and effectiveness in presenting in front of groups. Here are 3 that seem to target those fears and insecurities most of us feel when making a formal presentation:

- Accept your discomfort for what it is and don't fight it. The more you try to calm down, the more you are concentrating on the discomfort. Besides, that little bit of discomfort may be harnessed into energy and transformed into enthusiasm. Often times that nervousness is the result of believing that the audience is there to judge you when in fact they are there to receive what you have to offer. The audience is pulling for you. They want you to succeed.

- Admit you don't have all the answers. Being honest about your level of knowledge or limitations will also take some of the pressure off thinking you have to be perfect and all knowing. And, as the author says, it actually will increase your credibility.

- Practice, practice, practice. Prepared speeches need to be practiced and not just once. They need to be practiced until they are second nature. Recording your speech and then carefully analyzing your voice tone, gestures, fillers ("ah", "um") and eye contact will help in the delivery. Some suggest practicing your hand gestures and body movements during some of the critical points of the speech. (Should I open my hands or clasp them, should I pace or stand behind a lectern, where will pauses add the most impact?) Another idea is to use a mirror or a really good friend for feedback.

2. Practice when you are alone. There are also times when you may be asked to give an impromptu speech. These can throw off the best of speakers. What to say that is appropriate for the occasion and how to say it have to be just right. Here are a couple of tips for an impromptu talk:

- Practice impromptu speeches. Khoury (n.d.) suggests practicing each day when you are alone or with family or friend by selecting a topic of the day and give an impromptu speech about it. For example, have your spouse at dinner call out a topic and you respond with a 3 to 5 minutes presentation from your experience on the topic. Much of the discomfort from impromptu speeches is not necessarily the topic but the surprise of being asked to get up and offer your views on a subject. The more you become inoculated against that "surprise", the more natural your presentation will seem. And mentally you can concentrate on your response rather than the jitters you are feeling.

- Use a familiar pattern. Khoury also mentions having a pattern from which to organize your speech. One he suggests is F A T: Feelings, Anecdote, Tie-In. With this format you would open up the speech with some of your feelings regarding the topic, relate a personal anecdote or experience and close with tying the anecdote back to the original. At Toastmasters meetings the impromptu speech practice comes during "Table Topics". Any member can be asked to stand and give a 1 to 2-minute speech on any topic asked by the Table Topics Master. Using a prepared format helps organize your thoughts very quickly

3. More Practice. Ruby Mine (2013) has produced a fine product based on extemporaneous conversations called "Table Topics". It contains scores of cards asking various questions that when picked by the participant he or she speaks on the topics for a few minutes. It could be played in a group setting or individually as practice.

Protecting the Brand

Description

When protecting the brand, leaders act in ways to show that the reputation of the organization, work-group or job are of utmost importance. In order to do so the leader monitors information, as much as possible to correct or eliminate negative impressions, particularly as they are related to the public or clients. He connects communication both inside and outside the organization to the organization's vision or mission and personally believes in and states, in both written and verbal forms, the importance of the earned reputation. The leader maintains a "we really are the best" attitude in all communications dealing within and outside the organization.

Self-rating Scale

COMMAND: I have in place a plan for promoting the positive aspects of the work group or the organization as well as remind those inside the work group of the positive feedback from those outside the organization and how it is related to the vision or mission. I investigate and neutralize negative information inside the organization before it can be promoted outside the organization. If need be, I take corrective measures if they are needed to protect the organization's image. I uphold the belief that everyone, including myself, is accountable to the high standards set for work and interaction within the organization.

STRENGTH: I seek out how those inside and outside the organization view it and check on rumors or inaccurate information by trying to get to the source in order to adjust the information and work for improvement. I provide a counter view to any negative information using applicable data or other measures and have a general plan for protecting the image of the organization. I regularly remind those inside the organization of our high standards and how meeting those standards promotes a strong image to the community or clients.

CAPABLE: I actively/verbally defend the organization's image and reputation to others inside or outside the work group or organization and correct inaccurate information about the organization. I periodically remind others of the group's mission when dispelling rumors or correcting negative misunderstandings.

DEVELOPING: I take minimal steps to protect the image of the organization or work group. I really don't know what others inside or outside the organization say about it.

WEAKNESS: I can't say I put any concern into the reputation of the organization and am basically unaware of how those inside or outside view the organization or work group. When others address the negative view of the work group or organization, I counter the negative image.

Ways to Improve

1. **Look for origin of rumors**. Probably the most effective tool to protecting the image and reputation is to follow up on any rumor of misinformation that comes across your desk. Ignoring or discounting any negative information can build beyond your capacity at a later time to manage it. Tracking down the rumor's origin, whether it is misinformation or a targeted lie, has to be a priority whether you do it yourself or delegate it to a trusted peer or subordinate. Then, having identified where it started, that is where corrective measures are implemented and/or corrected privately. If it has gotten outside the business, it needs to be corrected publicly. Holding employees responsible for misinformation must also be part of the solution if they are the originator of the rumor. "It takes many good deeds to build a good reputation, and only one bad one to lose it."—Benjamin Franklin. Same is true of an unchallenged rumor.

2. **Model what you want**. Constant modelling of the business's core principals or mission is the most effective way to protect and safeguard the organization's

reputation. It is when the public sees a discrepancy between what a company publishes or believes and what is actually practiced that the reputation takes a hit. It is especially important that all of top management know, talk about and model the mission and vision statements. It is critical that the mission and vision statements be held to when dealing with a problem that has found its way outside the company involving clients or the public.

3. **Develop a crisis management plan**. Every organization, no matter the size, should have a public relations crisis management plan in place. Whether the crisis is public or internal a well-thought-out, written plan will help mitigate the damage to the reputation of the organization. It is crucial. Agnes (2016) identifies the 5 critical elements of an effective plan: activation guidelines, detailed action plans, a pre-approved crisis communication strategy and messaging, a thorough contacts list, and detailed resource repository which might include flow charts, areas of responsibility, emergency and private numbers, etc. Not having a plan or not regularly reviewing the plan with those responsible to carry it out

can only lead to chaos. If you don't have one, put a team together to research what one should look like and begin the process of writing one and making it part of the organization's training and culture

4. **Stay positive**. Positive communication both inside and outside the organization can stop several problems in their tracks before they have a chance to expand. Keeping all levels of the organization informed about the positive stories helps to nurture the kind of constructive climate that produces even more positive stories. That includes "Thank You" notes to clients, for example. Handing out letters of thanks and commendations for employee work well done is another. Testimonials that highlight the mission and vision of the company help to keep everyone centered. Keep the positive thoughts flowing.

5. **Regularly take the temperature of the organization.** Seek honest feedback about how the company is reacting to issues inside and outside the company structure. Whether this is done in conferences or with surveys, taking the feedback seriously and using it to further improve the reputation of the organization is a key to ongoing

identity management. As problems within those inventories are identified address them. Develop working groups to provide you with possible solutions and then implement those you can. Take the organization's temperature and apply the right medication when needed.

Searching for and Selecting Information
Description

Effective leaders gather and filter through all kinds of information related to their job, roles, expectations, subordinates, problems and more on a regular basis. This is especially true when trying to analyze the nature and complexity of a problem or implementing a new procedure. Strong leaders want all relevant information available before finally making a decision.

The nature of the data can include anything from hard, quantitative data to casual observation, even rumors. Everything related to a problem or proposal is collected and filtered so as to only deal with the most relevant pieces. Not only is there a significant breadth of search when gathering information, but also a significant depth in applicable categories or kinds. Competent leaders need and want to know what is going on and regularly sweep the formal and informal channels for information making conscious decisions about which information to use and which to discard.

There are three important reasons to gather relevant information:

- Gathering information begins the needed awareness of the factors influencing the health, climate and culture of the organization. This includes a careful review of the current conditions of area or policy of concern.
- Information establishes the needed credibility as decisions are made. Decisions pulled out of thin air are suspect and often incomplete and create unnecessary stress on the organization and its stakeholders.
- Conducting a broad search for data collection is critical when laying a solid foundation for change. Change is one of the most stressful factors affecting the climate of an organization. Sufficient, relevant data supporting change eases that stress and opens the lines of communication in order to move forward.

Self-rating Scale

COMMAND: I am very specific about the kind of information required of others and initiate searches for that data. I am comfortable filtering through information from multiple sources directly related to a problem and those that may be considered initially as tangential. I am quite capable at gathering data on multiple problems simultaneously easily and efficiently and can identify areas needing inquiry missed by others in a group situation. I respond to the input by others in a group dynamic with clarifying questions as needed. I am very clear as to why I use certain information but reject others.

STRENGTH: I search several areas with enough breadth or depth to make a sound decision and develop connections between areas searched. I effectively filter information, keeping and rejecting information pertinent to the problem and can explain why when asked. I have a good grasp on how others view the situation and what their positions are.

CAPABLE: I use all available information with regard to a work problem or proposal and begin to search some other areas for additional information but not all. The search is adequate but not always comprehensive. Occasionally information that may have affected the decision sometimes comes out after the decision is made. I make some selective decisions about which data or information to use but tend to accept most information. In group or team situations I listen more than ask questions of others for clarification.

DEVELOPING: I use openly available information regarding a problem but may request information in only one or two other sources. Inquiries are limited in both breadth and depth. Questioning is periodically used just to clarify another's position. I may select some information without a valid reason and filter ineffectively in many cases. I, at times, am at a loss to give a reasonable explanation as to why information was either accepted or rejected.

WEAKNESS: I show little or no concern for collecting information regarding a problem and have been known to make a decision without any inquiries for additional information. I feel insecure and may even have a lack of understanding about my own role and responsibilities. Sometimes my decisions are based on assumptions, not data or relevant information. I struggle to filter data according to its usefulness. I tend to accept and deal with any information gathered however limited, useful or broad.

Ways to Improve

1. **Try a fishbone**. Identifying the cause of any problem is the first step in selecting some solutions. If there is time for a thorough examination of the problem, the more input you have from stakeholders, data or observation, the better. When identifying the problem's causes, one very effective visual method is called the fishbone. It looks like this:

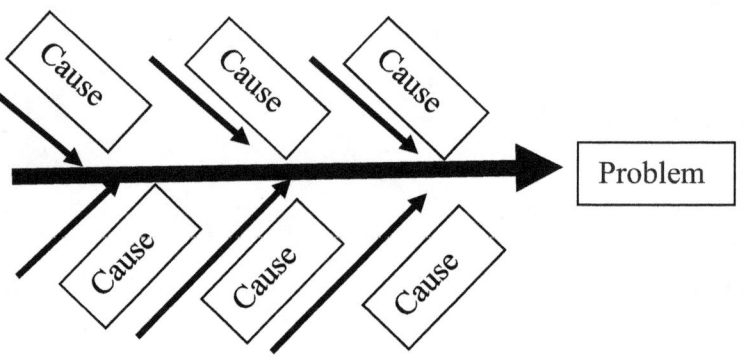

One suggestion is to write the causes on post-it notes and place them on a smart board or wall so that they can be moved around to fit into categories This is a very effective method in a group brainstorming meeting. Giving the group members the room for free thought to help solve the problem or create the policy is an added dividend.

2. **Have a plan on how to work with data**. Wharton@work (2015) identifies considerations when beginning to identify the factors in a problem:

- Don't be fooled by large amounts of data. Data isn't always the path to the solution, especially large, complex piles of impressive facts and figures.
- Dive below the surface to understand the system that underlies the problem. Observing the patterns that seem to be contributing factors to the problem isn't all there is to consider. Look below the patterns to find causes or sub-patterns. Working only with the surface indicators may well lead down the wrong path for a strong solution.
- Widen your focus. This is especially true when having to solve a problem involving personnel. Looking to solve a problem that exists with a single employee may not be the right answer for others employees, for example. Widen your scope and see the problem from several perspectives.

- Define the boundaries of the problem. In this step it is time to isolate only those factors, facts, or observations which are critical to the problem being solved. Identify the boundaries of the problem and those material factors within the boundaries. Eliminate all the others.
- Identify causes, effects, and key stakeholders. Once the boundaries are set it is time to deal with the causes, effects and key elements of the problem. Begin the process of categorizing, isolating and managing each of the internal factors including personnel.
- Analyze future developments. Once the analysis is complete, it is time to implement the solution and project into the future the outcomes to see if the problem is solved or if it could morph into something new. It is critical to the success of any major decision to forecast its effect on the organization's vital components

3. **Work with others**. Form a feedback group whose only purpose is to be absolutely honest in providing you information about any of the issues you might be facing.

This is the time for you to listen and take notes. It is a time to sit back and encourage thoughtful and direct communication from this team. Reassure them that whatever is said by whomever in the group is appreciated and confidential. The ideas, comments and suggestions are sacrosanct and privileged.

4. **Practice problem solving**. Petty, (2018) suggests a very novel approach to improve critical analysis and problem solving: adopt an orphan problem. That is, look for a problem in the organization that no one wants to deal with and adopt it as your own. Analyze it thoroughly, select information that is critical to understanding the status, begin considering solutions and project each possible solution looking for false positives. This is not only good practice but also shows those around you that you have what it takes to lead and follow through.

5. **Deconstruct a problem**. Key to selecting the facts or data which will help you come to the right solution to a problem is the ability to analyze information quickly, yet efficiently. Sharpening your analytical skills can be done through a variety of

ways: Top Universities (2016) writes about the importance of deconstructing a problem down to its components and then analyzing each of the components. They also highlight the importance of working in groups to solve a problem. Listening to other points of view and considering other avenues to solve a problem begin to build a vast storehouse of reference points for you to fall back on for future problems

6. Try on-line mind games. Terrell (n.d.) lists some ways to improve analytical skills including on line mind games like: Luminosity, Elevate, Eidetic, Wizard, Happify and Brain Wave. (More are being added as Apps every single day.) It was suggested also to volunteer for any new project. By virtue of engaging at the beginning of any new project or implementation it is almost assured there will be problems waiting to be discovered and solved.

Seeking Opinions from Others

Description

It is important that leaders understand the thoughts, likes, dislikes, and opinions of those with whom they are working. To do that leaders need to listen and ask for that information on a consistent basis. Strong leaders do not stop with just collecting those thoughts or opinions but can verbalize clearly that they understand. Active, not passive listening, is the hallmark of this competency.

As well, the other person's feelings are taken into consideration. A strong leader can verbalize the feelings of others (empathy). Techniques like probing, summarizing or paraphrasing, and brainstorming are tools to be used as needed in order to identify the rationale or personal perspective behind another person's decisions, sentiments or solutions. Strong leaders encourage others through targeted questioning and probing to expand on their ideas or concepts. Also, this is not gathering any concrete or factual information, per se, like the competency of Searching for and Selecting Information. The focus is on another's personal opinions, beliefs and preferences which may be based on their understanding the data or concrete information provided. Ideas, hunches, feelings of others are important to thoroughly and honestly access and process.

Self-rating Scale

COMMAND: I often ask others for their opinions when faced with a decision and do so before the decision is made. I really want as many opinions as possible from as many people affected as possible as they apply to the pending problem or decision. I use a variety of techniques in order to get others to give me a full and complete understanding of their ideas or rationale. And I listen very attentively and restate what I understand to be their opinion to ensure that I have it. I utilize a variety of techniques in order to draw out honest opinions and ideas.

STRENGTH: I often ask for opinions but too often limit it to a single person. I do let others know that their opinions are important and can influence the final decision. I am familiar with and often use open-ended probes, summarizing, paraphrasing or other techniques to get participants to clarify their opinions or ideas.

CAPABLE: I may seek out the opinion of only one person when considering a decision on a single issue. Sometimes I will ask questions so as to clarify their ideas or opinions, but not always.

DEVELOPING: The opinions of others is not a priority, though I will listen if advanced by another person. Honestly, I often make the decision without first consulting others, but will thank them for their ideas later.

WEAKNESS: I do not actively seek out the opinions of others affected by an upcoming decision.

Ways to Improve

1. **Watch for "mutual deception"**. Freedman (2017) warns about "on the surface" communication: "How are you?" "I'm fine. How about you?" "Yep fine. Have a good day." He calls it "mutual deception". There has been no real exchange of information or communication. He writes, "If you want to understand others, you need to get beneath the surface and start understanding emotions. If you fool yourself into believing the surface story, you're missing invaluable data." In order to have a real conversation that involves feelings, there are 3 considerations which much be attended to: safety, speed and script:

- Safety accounts for the need for absolute trust. Freedman suggests building that trust by asking a question that matches the present trust level. The next conversation might begin with a question which raises the level of trust and so on until a firm foundation of trust and safety are established. When doing so, plan for privacy and time needed to listen.

- Second, speed deals with the time needed to allow for a thorough exploration of how the person feels. Don't ask a question that could lead to an hour discussion if you only have 5 minutes.
- Last, script is about the flow of the conversation. Take turns sharing, asking, listening, recognizing, and reflecting. As the dialogue flows back and forth, it also flows beyond the surface. Listen more than you talk or respond, for example.

2. **Empathy and agreement are not the same always**. It is important to internalize that showing empathy and sympathy toward a person does not mean that you agree with their feelings. You can still show empathy and understanding without supporting the reasons for how they are feeling. For example, if a client feels she was treated badly by an employee and heatedly describes in detail what happened, you can show you care but not agree with his or her memories or description. Remember, the perception of what happened may not include all the detail. A response like, "If I was treated like that, I would probably feel the same way. What you described to me was

very inconsiderate." Nowhere in that response have you agreed to that client's recollection. You have just acknowledged it. It doesn't generally leave any room for further anger. And once the anger subsides then the facts can be introduced. Practicing responses which acknowledge feelings but leave room for further exploration will go a long way in resolving problems.

3. **Learn to read body language**. Stok (2017) lists what kinds of information about feelings can be gleaned just by being observant.

Examples of Physical Communication:

Body Part	Meaning That Can Noticed
Face	Emotions
Shoulders	Stress Level
Arms	Mood
Hands	Despite cultural differences, hands can illustrate thoughts (see table below).
Legs	Despite upbringing and gender differences, leg positions can indicate comfort, disinterest or insecurity.

Non-verbal Communication Through the Hands

Hand Gestures	Non-verbal Communication
Clenched Fist	Anger
Hands in Pockets	Meaningless
Hands Held	Confused

4. **Asking the right question is important**. Coleman in his article, *Asking for Opinions 101*, offers 4 suggestions that will help you keep an open mind:

- First, make sure an opinion is what you actually want. Don't confuse asking for someone's thoughts about an issue if really you are fishing for a compliment or encouragement. There is nothing wrong with looking for support or a good word, but if that is the reason for the conversation, be honest about it. If you want an opinion, then clear the air sufficiently so the people responding know you want to hear their thoughts regardless.

- Next, if you are going to ask for an opinion be sure you have the stomach to hear what is said. "When you treat constructive criticism as an attack, you lose in two major ways: you stop learning and you build a reputation for being someone who can't handle the truth which results in people withholding from you the very truths you need to know in order to succeed."

- Third, make sure you are asking the person that you respect. There are people in your life whose opinions have weight and others whose opinions are fluff. Know the difference and go to the person who has the expertise and knowledge to offer solid feedback.
- Last, be willing to take the advice despite the way it is delivered. Some people can be brutally honest. Others are quick to the point while still others deliver in sermon format. Everyone is different which is a good thing. Plan for the setting and the time to listen and accept the information while allowing the person the space to provide it in any way he or she likes.

5. **Is it the right question?** Preparing the proper question will go a long way in receiving valuable feedback. Write out some questions that will not only open up the conversation, but target exactly the information you want. For example, "I have

been thinking about expanding our company in this area. I'm not sure it's good move and I really value your experience. What do you think?" Or, "I have been trying some new ways to manage personnel. I am wondering if you or anyone else has noticed any differences. Could you fill me in on what you have or haven't seen and how you feel about any change you have seen?" Wording and timing—thought out beforehand—will make a lot of difference in the quality of the response.

"Take-Charge" Mentality

Description

Effective leaders act out of the belief that they are fully in charge and responsible for what happens in a situation or on the job even if it is not under their assigned duties. They are hands-on rather than reactive. Often this mindset is characterized by the leader using the word "I", as in: "I saw...","I felt...", "I decided...". He or she sees him or herself as the "cause" or stimulus to move the organization forward and reach organizational goals or outcomes. These leaders look for opportunities to act and then devise plans to optimize those opportunities.

Take-charge leaders take responsibility for success or failure in task accomplishment but learn from those experiences and apply that learning to future problems or opportunities. They also look for ways to preempt problems. They often initiate the events or actions for themselves and others by structuring the goals, tasks, or processes/projects as well as the approach to solve the problem or achieve the desired goal. Typically, leaders with high "take-charge" mentality are organized and schedule meetings, define the agenda; gather support; take actions that focus others on the task at hand; and establish a plan of action with assignments and time-tables. In other words, proactive, take-charge, hands-on leaders see the problem, take on the responsibility for what needs to be done and develop a plan to accomplish it.

Self-rating Scale

COMMAND: I often initiate or develop detailed plans for the organization's or group's future and take responsibility for its overall success or failure. I find people to help or gain compliance from others, and then establish a process with concrete actions or steps. After I develop the agenda, I call meetings specifically to share the plan, responsibilities and time lines. I take steps to keep the group focused on the task when needed in order to keep things moving. If I see a problem, I just naturally feel it is my role to fix it.

STRENGTH: I initiate actions or plans as needed if I see there aren't any. Before a meeting concludes I make sure there is a plan of action in place by giving direction and/or assigning responsibilities to the group or individuals in the group. I feel I have to keep others on task once a plan is established. If I see a problem, whether it's part of my job or not, I look for ways to solve it and bring it to the attention of those who can help.

CAPABLE: I show an awareness for the need to take responsibility when I see a problem. Sometimes I might give some direction to others or suggest a general outline of a plausible plan or solution to a problem.

DEVELOPING: I see and verbalize the need for a plan to accomplish a goal or create a solution but don't take the initiative to see it through. I am not comfortable establishing a possible direction or solution when the problem is identified. Honestly, sometimes I can't say I have a concern for the future impact of plan or solution or even the possible recurrence of the problem.

WEAKNESS: I don't feel it is my responsibility to develop plans, assign resources etc. I am more focused on my own view, or reasons why things don't get done. Sometimes I outwardly state I feel that a situation is hopeless.

Ways to Improve

1. **Five steps to consider**. Scivicque (2010) identifies 5 steps that need to be considered in order to develop a proactive management style.

- **Predict**-. Always look for and read the tea leaves of your organization. Anticipating a problem is the best defense against managing a problem. Use your logic, reason and creative mind to predict possible issues. Develop a sense of foresight.
- **Prevent**- What are some possible plans that will divert or minimize the influence of the perceived problem preventing it from becoming a roadblock.
- **Plan**. Proactive people are always thinking ahead and mentally outlining plans to get where they want to go. "Don't make decisions in a vacuum; every decision is a link in a chain of events leading to one final conclusion. In order to make the best decision, you have to know where you came from, where you are, and where you want to end up".

- **Participate**. Get involved— engage and contribute. Use your influence and experience with others.
- **Perform**. Take the initiative and become active.

2. **Use your feedback**. Feedback is important not only to tell you how you are doing, but you can also find developing patterns that need your attention. Feedback from surveys, data collections, observation, employee conversations can all provide pieces of a yet-to-be-seen problem. Seek out as much information as possible from as many sources as possible. Plan as many ways as possible to collect and organize it. Its variety and depth can yield a great deal of information.

3. **Consider having a mentor**. Developing any personal skill or trait is much easier if you find others who already good at that trait and watch what they do. Finding a mentor is a solid way to develop a new skill. Most experienced managers are very willing to develop others in the organization. Sometimes you have to be a little proactive in order to become proactive by seeking out and asking that person you hope to

become to give you some of their time and wisdom.

3. Practice going after problems. Take-charge managers have that mindset regardless of the status or complexity of the problem. In other words, proactive managers look at discovering and solving a small irritating problem with the same intensity as they do one that could destroy the company. Take-charge people are always on stage looking for something to fix. Don't wait for a big problem to solve, begin with finding the small, irritating problems. Swatting a business mosquito often times is just as helpful as slaying the dragon.

4. **Become familiar with failure.** People who take charge are not usually discouraged by failure. Failure is a forerunner to success. Mistakes and setbacks are part of the game if you are going to assume leadership. Mistakes are learning opportunities and setbacks allow for reflection. Accept failure just as readily as you do success. Teach those around you as well that any misstep can still be a path forward. Fear of failure is a roadblock to developing a proactive mindset and must be overcome.

5. **Monitor your language**. Proactive people use "I" as a statement of willingness and availability: "I will.", "I can.", "I volunteer." And reactive people use statements like, "If only ...", "I have to ...", I think...". Use strong statements that project your capacity to solve problems. Not only act like you are in charge, but remind others through your language that you **are** in charge and responsible.

Weighing Multiple Ideas and Concepts
Description

Strong leaders know that events or problems have multiple parts and must be viewed from multiple perspectives simultaneously in order to mentally organize or evaluate them, also referred to as "cognitive flexibility". Therefore, leaders manipulate competing models or concepts mentally at the same time while moving toward a decision. This skill is characterized by the leader simultaneously considering the critical attributes as well as pros and cons of each and every perspective and their implications for a solution. All opinions and perspectives remain active up to the final decision. No perspectives are deleted out of hand.

Decisions are finalized after thoroughly considering arguments for and against and implications of each conflicting or competing idea. Data is very important in building ideas or concepts and used when choosing a final solution. In group discussions, a strong leader keeps everyone's perspectives and concepts viable and can precisely summarize the pertinent aspects of each person's position as the discussion moves forward toward a solution set.

Categorizing or evaluating ideas and concepts often leads to new and creative solutions. Limitations are set aside and divergent thinking is engaged. Comparing and contrasting all available ideas or concepts offer insight and promote progress toward final conclusions.

Self-rating Scale

COMMAND: I am comfortable weighing the "fit" of several relevant yet competing alternatives or concepts as they relate to a present problem or decision. As part of the process I mentally manipulate the information from each alternative while working through the decision-making process. I believe in data as a marker in decision-making and utilize it as often as possible in the final decision. Sometimes I make a decision by selecting the best pieces of each alternative to form a completely new alternative.

In group processes I ask members to look for connections among alternatives and to highlight them for consideration. All alternatives are kept in focus for myself and others. I am most comfortable forming a hypothesis using data and most satisfied with data-driven decisions. The organization's mission is considered as part of the final solution.

STRENGTH: I can easily analyze two alternative concepts simultaneously when facing a decision. The positives and negatives of each one and the predicted outcomes based on those pros and cons for each one, are considered. As needed, I verbalize the possible consequences of alternating views both in the short term and long term and use the information from each alternative diagnostically. I make decisions based on the relative weights of pros and cons. Data is seen as an important factor to consider.

CAPABLE: I can work with two alternative concepts simultaneously (clearly differentiated and independent) when facing a decision and move to understand the details of alternative perspectives provided by others. I can verbalize the importance of those alternative ideas but don't work to find connections between competing ideas before making a decision regardless of whether they are my suggestions or those from someone else. I accept the data if any is available.

DEVELOPING: Decisions are based on a single concept's pros and cons. I am aware of other concepts but little consideration is given toward their value and connections to the decision at hand.

WEAKNESS: I tend to maintain my own biases in a situation or preconceived ideas and base my decision on them.

Honestly, opinions, ideas, concepts of others are dismissed or ignored

Ways to Improve

1. **Choose the right tool**. Gonsenhauser (2017) lays out 5 very simplistic steps when confronted with analyzing a problem. First, clearly define the problem Second, what proof is there that the problem exists? Third, establish its impact on the organization. Fourth, establish probable causes. And last, reverse the causes.

2. **How do you word the problem**? One way to understand the problem and thus create a number of solutions is in the wording of the problem itself. Try rewriting the problem in as many ways as you can create. Get together some of the people connected with the problem to help generate as many angles as possible and write them all down as different ways to perceive it. Change the words and the ways the words express the problem.

3. **What are the presuppositions**? Every problem has a set of assumptions or perceived limitations attached to it. Write down what you believe are the "givens" to the problem and then begin the process of challenging each one. The very things you take for granted as being true are the ones

which need to be challenged. Because assumptions presuppose outcomes, once they are challenged it opens up new ideas and other outcomes.

4. **Isolate complex problems and their respective components**. Throughout the day a leader or manager could easily find several competing problems and it can easily overwhelm the brain's capacity to organize and differentiate them. It is helpful to put each problem, contributing factor or solution into its own box, if you will, so that you can deal with each one separately. One suggestion is to give each one a different file folder and then as thoughts, data, possible solutions emerge write them on the file folder or on a sticky note and stick them to the inside of the folder. Physically separating each problem, contributing factor or solution will help to keep the channels of thought open for each and reduce any possible confusion.

5. **Consider a crisis solution team**. Create a crisis solution team whose responsibility it is to generate as many solutions as possible for consideration to meet the demands of an immediate problem. The team not only helps identity the

components of the problem, but in generating solutions lists the pro and cons for each one. The most effective way to organize it is by writing out each idea or solution and then sticky-note under it all the pros and cons. Ask the team to use their foresight, so as to predict any future needs created by any one of the solutions. A crisis team can help you as a leader manage the data, the probable solutions and predict the success of each one.

Writing for Effect
Description

Writing well and with purpose is important. This is more than writing lists or notations. It includes well thought out, carefully constructed composition. Leaders must be able to put their ideas and/or orders into written form with appropriate style, syntax, grammar, spelling and meaning, adjusting the comprehension level as needed for the intended audience. He or she uses the accepted standards for writing such as short sentences; limited length of the first paragraph; and strong, rich words conveying the needed tone or "voice" as appropriate. Proof reading for errors; assuring a clear, understandable message; and checking the overall quality of any written communication are particularly important in this age of immediate distribution using electronic platforms like email.

Self-rating Scale

COMMAND: My written communication is almost always error free. I tailor my grammar, syntax, work choice and style on the audience. I also work to develop the written communication skills of those under my direction as needed, but generally not evaluative unless it is part of the formal evaluation model for that subordinate. I strongly believe that my ability to write well is not only a reflection of my own growth and capabilities but also reflects on the organization. Writing well must be attended to.

STRENGTH: I am a good writer. Attention to the conventions of good writing is obvious in all of my work and most work is error free. The level and understanding of the reader are considered. My writing shows a varied and fairly strong use of vocabulary. Consistency and quality are carefully monitored using available software or other resources.

CAPABLE: I use written communication comfortably and am aware of the requirements or minimal standards of quality before sending it to its intended audience.

Care is taken to meet the standards of quality writing though proof-reading though that too can sometimes prove to be inadequate. When I am rushed, I delegate proof-reading to another member of the staff to help ensure quality.

DEVELOPING: I use written communication only as needed or required, but work to make attempts acceptable to the audience for which it is intended.

WEAKNESS: Writing formally is not my strength and I choose to do very little or no writing in my work position. Samples of my attempts of writing show errors in word use, grammar, punctuation, proof-reading and so on.

Ways to Improve

1. **Take a class**. Probably the most practical suggestion is to take a writing course. There are several on-line from which to choose. They are inexpensive and the feedback could be invaluable as you work to improve your wording, syntax and expression. One such course is conducted by the bloggers of *"The Minimalist"*. (https://www.theminimalists.com/class/)

2. **A proof reader is invaluable**. Make sure that you have a proof reader for anything that is going out to superiors. Find someone you can trust not only to be truthful with you about your writing, but also understands the term "confidential" when needed. It truly only takes a single misplaced word to change the whole tone and impression of a note, email or resume. And the truth is we are not our own best editors.

3. **Stick with simplicity**. Don't write above your own understanding of the nuances of words. Trying to use the thesaurus as a way to impress the recipient of a letter can certainly lead to misunderstanding as well. Often times it is best to use the simplest ways to express yourself rather than

trying to impress the reader with multi-syllabic words that are all too often only used in certain contexts. Keep it simple.

Most word processing programs have a text reader that generates the grade level equivalent of a piece of narrative. Use it. It is common to see on the internet that many magazine and newspapers rarely meet the 8th grade level reading proficiency.

4. **Paragraphs have a purpose**. It goes without saying that paragraphs are composed of sentences that support the main idea of the paragraph—usually the introductory sentence. Too often in writing, the writers divide up paragraphs by size and pay no attention to the content of each. Each sentence in a paragraph points to the topic sentence of that paragraph and it is generally accepted that each paragraph has at least 3 supporting sentences. All the paragraphs make up the script of the text and when done properly it naturally flows. Watch the use of sentences and building paragraphs.

5. **Walk away**. Walk away from your email or letter and do something else and then come back and read it again if there is time. When we self-edit, most are pretty

good at finding the typos and missing punctuation, but when reading the content our brains often deceive us. Because we know how a sentence is supposed to read, we will read into it any missing words. Our brain supplies what's missing and we never see the error when proof reading. Walking away to attend to some other task is a good way to reset the brain. Giving yourself time to refresh will catch what you might never see if you proof your work right after writing it.

Bibliography/References

Adler, M. (2018). *Emotional Intelligence: How Good Leaders Become Great.* YouTube. https://www.youtube.com/watch?v=HA15YZlF_kM.

Agnes, M. (May 3, 2016), *5 "Must Include" Items for your Crisis Management Plan.* https://melissaagnes.com/5-must-include-items-for-your-crisis-managment-plan/ .

Bariso, J. (n.d.). *13 Signs of High Emotional Intelligence.* https://www.inc.com/justin-bariso/13-things-emotionally-intelligent-people-do.html

Berglas, S. (Jan 11, 2013). *The Top 5 Ways to Manage Closed-Minded, Defensive, Truth-Resistant People.* https://www.forbes.com/sites/stevenberglas/2013/01/11/the-top-5-ways-to-manage-closed-minded-defensive-truth-resistant-people/?sh=467a5e8660f8)

Bergman, P. (June 14, 2012). *The Essential Adventure of Leadership.* http://mtntactical.com/knowledge/what-does-it-mean-to-be-a-quiet-professional/

Carniol, A. (October 23, 2018); *Tips on How to Prioritize, Organize, and Plan Your Work*, https://www.interviewsuccessformula.com/job-search-advice/tips-on-how-to-prioritize-organize-and-plan-your-work.php .

CBS News (Sept .14, 2010). *Action Video Games Found to Sharpen Decision-Making.* https://www.cbsnews.com/news/action-video-games-found-to-sharpen-decision-making/ .

Changing Minds (ND). Groups. http://changingminds.org/explanations/groups/groups.htm.

Coleman, T (n.d.). *Asking for an Opinion 101.* https://discoverpraxis.com/asking-for-an-opinion-101/ .

DeMaio, S. (September 16, 2009). *The Art of Giving Praise.* https://hbr.org/2009/09/the-art-of-giving-praise.html .

DeMers, J. (n.d.) *7 Strategies to Delegate Better and Get More Done.* https://www.inc.com/jayson-demers/7-strategies-to-delegate-better-and-get-more-done.html .

Fabrega, M. (2018). "How to Learn from Your Mistakes".
https://daringtolivefully.com/learn-from-your-mistakes.

Fessler, L. (April 26, 2020) *"You're no genius": Her father's shutdowns made Angela Duckworth a world expert on grit.* https://qz.com/work/1233940/angela-duckworth-explains-grit-is-the-key-to-success-and-self-confidence/

Fishback, A., Ayel,T., & Finelstein.S. (2010). How Positive and Negative Feedback Motivate Goal Pursuit. Social and Personality Psychology Compass. *Social and Personality Psychology Compass*, 4/8, 517-530.

Find Law (n.d.). *Monitoring Employees.* https://smallbusiness.findlaw.com/employment-law-and-human-resources/monitoring-employees.html .

Folkman, J. (March 20, 2013). *Everything Counts: The 6 Ways to Inspire and Motivate Top Performance.*
https://www.forbes.com/sites/joefolkman/2013/05/20/everything-counts-the-6-ways-to-inspire-and-motivate-top-performance/#3e0ba8ed25e1 .

Folkman, J. (Sept. 19, 2013). *Solving the Decisiveness Dilemma: The 4 Step Process for Making an Excellent Choice.* Forbes https://www.forbes.com/sites/joefolkman/2013/09/19/solving-the-decisiveness-dilemma-the-4-step-process-for-making-an-excellent-choice/#572fac021a15 .

Freedman, J. (April 13, 2017). *How to Understand People: Ask, Listen, and Get Real.*
https://www.6seconds.org/2017/04/13/feelings-communication-relationship/.

Fripp, P. (n.d.): Public *Speaking- The Importance of the Pause.*
https://www.fripp.com/the-importance-of-the-pause/ .

Frost, A. (n.d.). *To Be a Great Leader, Ask Questions. Don't Answer Them.*
https://www.themuse.com/advice/to-be-a-great-leader-ask-questions-dont-answer-them .

GCF Global (n.d.) *10 Creative Presentation Ideas: That Will Inspire Your Audience to Action.*
https://business.tutsplus.com/tutorials/creative-presentation-ideas--cms-27281.

Giles, S. (March 15, 2016). *The Most Important Leadership Competencies According to Leaders Around the World.* https://www.entrepreneur.com/article/295298..

Glei, J (2018). *Why You Need "White Space" in Your Daily Routine.* https://jkglei.com/white-space/

Goleman, D. (Dec., 2013). *The Focused Leader.*
https://hbr.org/2013/12/the-focused-leader .

Gonsenhauser, A. (Feb. 2017). *Five Easy Steps to Analyze Any Problem.* https://www.forrester.com/blogs/fiveeasystepstoanalyzeanyproblem/ .

Hawkins, H. (Nov. 26, 2013). Commitment to Mission, Vision, & Values: The Third Attribute of Positive Leaders. *https://melhawkinsandassociates.com/commitment-to-mission-vision-values-the-third-attribute-of-positive-leaders/* .

Heathfield, S. (Jan 1, 2018). *Use Coaching to Improve Employee Performance.* https://www.thebalancecareers.com/use-coaching-to-improve-employee-performance-1918083 .

Hicks, A. (March 10, 2017); *Top 10 Ways to Improve Employee Efficiency.* https://www.zenefits.com/blog/top-10-ways-to-improve-employee-efficiency/ .

Hoffeld, D. (2015). *Four Counterintuitive Habits of Effective Leaders.* https://www.fastcompany.com/3054273/four-counterintuitive-habits-of-effective-leaders.

How to Persuade Different People. (n.d). https://www.eruptingmind.com/how-to-persuade-different-types-of-people/ .

Kay, M. (June 2, 2016), *Tips for Communication Skills with Groups.* https://aboutleaders.com/tips-for-communication-skills-with-groups/#gs.Hb42qTE .

Keiling, H (October 11, 2021). 83 Core Value Examples for the Workplace. https://www.indeed.com/career-advice/career-development/core-values .)

Kim, L. (April 13, 2018), *20 Ways to Improve Your Presentation Skills*; https://www.wordstream.com/blog/ws/2014/11/19/how-to-improve-presentation-skills .

Khoury, P (n.d.). *How to Give an Impressive Impromptu Speech.* https://magneticspeaking.com/how-to-give-an-impressive-impromptu-speech/ .

Kruse, K. (July 19, 2017). Persuade Me: The Two Keys to Convincing People. https://www.forbes.com/sites/kevinkruse/2017/07/19/persuade-me-the-two-keys-to-convincing-people/#86e846f62a80 .

Laurinavicius, T. (Dec. 6, 2017) *Reasons Why Writing is a Critical Skill for Success.*

https://www.huffingtonpost.com/tomas-laurinavicius/reasons-why-writing-remai_b_12701380.html .

Ledden, E. (Feb 16, 2017). *Master the Art of Presenting: Tell a Story, Keep it Brief.* https://www.theguardian.com/small-business-network/2017/feb/16/master-art-presenting-tell-story-brief-audience .

Limeade Marketing. (April 18, 2014). *8 Ways to Communicate Change to Employees,*

https://www.limeade.com/2014/04/8-ways-to-communicate-change-to-employees/ .

Loehr, A. (April 26, 2018); *How to Influence Others Without Authority*; https://www.anneloehr.com/2018/04/26/how-to-influence-others/ .

Manpower Experis. (n.d.) *Strengthening Your Decisiveness Ability.* https://www.experisjobs.us/exp_us/en/career-advice/strengthening-your-decisiveness-ability.htm .

Manageris. (2018). *The Intuitive Leader.* https://www.manageris.com/synopsis-the-intuitive-leader-20403.html .

Marcus, B. (Sept. 1, 2015). *Intuition is an Essential Leadership Tool.* https://www.forbes.com/sites/bonniemarcus/2015/09/01/intuiton-is-an-essential-leadership-tool/#46d1e461c188

Martin. (March 4, 2018). *How to Persuade Different Types of People.* Erupting Mind. https://www.eruptingmind.com/how-to-persuade-different-types-of-people/

Martinuzzi, B. (n.d.). *Laugh Track: How Humor Can Enhance Employee Productivity.* https://www.americanexpress.com/us/small-business/openforum/articles/humor/ .

Maxwell, J. (2007). *The 21 Irrefutable Laws of Leadership*. Nashville: Thomas Nelson Publishers.

McGraw, P. (Oct. 12, 2010). *What Makes Things Funny?* https://www.youtube.com/watch?v=ysSgG5V-R3U .

Melymbrose, J. (Sept 22, 2016). *10 Creative Presentation Ideas: That Will Inspire Your Audience to Action.*

https://business.tutsplus.com/tutorials/creative-presentation-ideas--cms-27281.

Minors, P. (n.d.). *Grit by Angela Duckworth [Book Summary and PDF].* https://paulminors.com/grit-angela-duckworth-book-summary-pdf/#boxzilla-37360 .

Ogden, N. (March 28, 2016). *How Emotions Can Support Critical Thinking.* https://ww2.kqed.org/education/2016/03/28/how-emotions-can-support-critical-thinking/

Petty, A. (August 21, 2018); *6 Exercises to Strengthen Your Critical Thinking Skills.* https://www.thebalancecareers.com/strengthen-critical-thinking-skills-2275911 .

Porter, T. & Schumann, K. (2018). *Intellectual humility and openness to the opposing view.* Self and Identity, 17, 139-162.

Posner, B & Kouzes, J. (Aug 2, 2017) *The Five Practices of Exemplary Leadership.* https://www.success.com/article/5-practices-of-exemplary-leadership .

Price, R. (May 2016). *Everyday Management*: Tips for Busy Leaders. https://www.thecompleteleader.org/blog/everyday-management-tips-busy-leaders .

Rick, T. (June 14, 2011). *20 Tips to Improve Employee Engagement and Performance.*

https://www.torbenrick.eu/blog/performance-management/20-tips-to-improve-employee-engagement-and-performance/ .

Rise Staff (May 1, 2018). *7 Eye-opening Strategies to Improve Employee Performance.*

https://risepeople.com/blog/7-steps-improving-employee-performance-2/ .

Ryan, John. (no date). *Decisiveness. One of the Most Important Leadership Traits.*

https://www.johnryanleadership.com/decisiveness-one-of-the-most-important-leadership-traits/)

Scivicque, C. (August 30, 2010). *How to Be Proactive at Work: My 5 Step System.* https://www.eatyourcareer.com/2010/08/how-be-proactive-at-work-step-system/ .

Sehgal, K. (Nov 22, 2016). *How to Write Email with Military Precision.* https://getpocket.com/explore/item/how-to-write-email-with-military-precision .

Shallcross, L. (Feb 14, 2010). *Managing Resistant Clients.*

https://ct.counseling.org/2010/02/managing-resistant-clients/ .

Shaul, R. (Oct. 15, 2015). *The Quiet Professional.*

http://mtntactical.com/knowledge/what-does-it-mean-to-be-a-quiet-professional .

Simmons, R. (1995). *Control in an Age of Empowerment.*
https://hbr.org/1995/03/control-in-an-age-of-empowerment.

Smith, J. (May, 2013). *How to Be a Great Mentor.* https://www.forbes.com/sites/jacquelyn-smith/2013/05/17/how-to-become-a-great-mentor/#26b13494f599 .

Smith, P. (2012). Lead with a Story. AMACOM: New York.

South Dakota School Mines and Technology (n.d.). *Understanding Group Process.* Student Activities and Leadership Center. https://www.sdsmt.edu/uploaded-Files/Content/Campus_Life/Student_Activities/Organizations/Understanding%20Group%20Process.pdf .

Stok, G. (Dec. 27, 2017). *How to Understand and Feel What Someone Else Is Feeling*;

https://pairedlife.com/relationships/How-To-Understand-By-Listening-To-Meaning .

Surdek, S. (Nov. 17, 2016). *Why Understanding Other Perspectives Is A Key Leadership Skill.* Forbes. https://www.forbes.com/sites/forbescoachescouncil/2016/11/17/why-understanding-other-perspectives-is-a-key-leadership-skill/#c07e3cf6d206 .

Sutton, J. (Sept 12, 2021). *15 Ways to Give Negative Feedback, Positively (Incl. Examples).* Positive Psychology Today. https://positivepsychology.com/negative-feedback/

Ruby Mine. (2013). *Table Topics. Questions to Start Great Conversations.* Available for purchase at www.tabletopics.com .

Terrell, S. (n.d.) *5 Ways to Improve and Expand Your Analytical Thinking Skills.* https://blog.mindvalley.com/analytical-thinking-skills/?utm_source=google_blog .

Top Universities. (May 12, 2016). *How to Improve Your Analytical Skills.* https://www.topuniversities.com/blog/how-improve-your-analytical-skills .

Watson, S. (July 10, 2010*). 10 Tips for Effective Workplace Communication.* https://money.howstuffworks.com/business/starting-a-job/10-tips-for-effective-workplace-communication.htm ./

Wharton@Work (June 2015). *Better Decision-Making: Identify the Real Problem.* https://executiveeducation.wharton.upenn.edu/thought-leadership/wharton-at-work/2015/06/identify-the-real-problem/ .

Winerman, L. (Nov. 2005). *Where Did that Idea Come From?* http://www.apa.org/monitor/nov05/idea.aspx .

Young, S. (March, 2007). *Be Decisive.* https://www.scotthyoung.com/blog/2007/03/19/be-decisive/ .

Zipkin, N. (June 2, 2017). *Want to Build Relationships? Find Ways to Laugh Together.*

https://www.entr0epreneur.com/article/295298 .

www.ingramcontent.com/pod-product-compliance
Lightning Source LLC
Chambersburg PA
CBHW061323040426
42444CB00011B/2749